pretty simple cocktails

JULIANNA MCINTOSH

pretty simple
cocktails

MARGARITAS, MOCKTAILS,
SPRITZES, AND MORE

FOR EVERY MOOD AND OCCASION

PHOTOGRAPHS BY LUCIANNA MCINTOSH

 CLARKSON POTTER/PUBLISHERS
NEW YORK

Contents

INTRODUCTION   6

Pretty Simple Essentials 9

How to Think (and Drink) Seasonally	10
The Elements of a Great Cocktail	12
Stocking the Bar of Your Dreams	14
Home Bar Essential Tools	18
Conversion Cheat Sheet	20
Essential Glassware	22
Ice. It Matters.	26
A Guide to Garnishing	28

Relaxed Refreshers 32

The Verde Maria	35
Breakfast of Champions	36
Bourbon & Basil Smash	39
Rhubarb & Cognac Fizz	40
Lemon Prosecco Pops	43
Jules's Piña Colada	44
The Pink Daiquiri	47
Frozen Peach Palmer	48
Lillet Highball	51
Kumquat Kick	52
Spicy Watermelon Punch	55

Spritz Is a State of Mind 56

Jules's Aperol Spritz	58
Limoncello Spritz	61
Fro-secco Spritz	62
The Apple-rol Spritz	65
Winter Sbagliato	66
Bianco Spritz	69
Sunset Spritz	70
Rosé All Day Spritz Punch	73
Citrus Party Punch Spritz	74

A Margarita for Every Mood 76

Classic Margarita	78
Coconut Aperol Margarita	81
Pineapple Mezcal Margarita	82
Avocado Margarita	85
Carrot Margarita	86
Blended Tropical Margarita	89
The Paloma-rita Sour	90
Blood Orange Thyme Margarita	93
Pantry Margarita	94
Tangy Tamarind Punch	97

4

Start the Party on a High Note 98

Olive Oil Martini 100
Apricot French 75 103
Passion Fruit Martini 104
Kentucky Jungle Bird 107
Smoked Rosemary Negroni Sour 108
Lychee Martini 111
Stone Fruit Whiskey Sour 112
Persimmon Mezcal Sour 115
The Vacationer's Last Word 116
The Weekenders' Party Punch 119
Winter Spice Sangria 120

Drinks for Cozy Occasions 122

La Dolce Vita 125
Pumpkin-Spiced Irish Coffee 126
Freezer Door Manhattan 129
Après Ski Hot Chocolate 130
Tiramisu Espresso-tini 133
Lemon Meringue Martini 134
Nonna's Tom & Jerry 137
Homemade Citrus-cello 138

Booze-Free Beauties 140

Orange Dreamsicle 143
Free Spirit Spritz 144
Booze-Free Margarita 147
Minus the Gin & Tonic 148
Melon No-jito 151
Nonalcoholic Carajillo 152
Tiki Tiki Tiki Room 155
Garden Refresher Punch 156

Pretty Simples and Shrubs 158

Plain Simple Syrup 160
Honey Syrup 160
Strawberry Syrup 161
Cherry Syrup 161
Herbaceous Syrups 162
Pumpkin Spice Syrup 162
Cinnamon Syrup 163
Vanilla Syrup 163
Vanilla & Cinnamon Syrup 163
Orange Zest Syrup 164
Prosecco Syrup 164
Cucumber Syrup 165
Persimmon Syrup 165
Spicy Pepper Syrup 166
Cranberry Syrup 166
Rhubarb Shrub 167
Chile Liqueur 167
Simple Cocktails Chart 168

DRINK YOUR SEASONS 169

DRINKS BY SPECIALTY SPIRIT 169

ACKNOWLEDGMENTS 170

INDEX 172

If you're reading this, it's probably safe to assume that you appreciate a good cocktail. Maybe you've been shaking up drinks for decades, or maybe you're just starting to set up the bar of your dreams in your first apartment. Whoever you are, welcome to the party—we've got plenty of booze, bubbles, and mocktails to go around.

If you're used to ordering cocktails from professionals (aka mixologists or your best friend who is really into home bartending), mixing a drink can seem mysterious and even intimidating. But as I've learned, you don't need a commercially stocked bar full of specialty liqueurs and bitters (or even any crazy tools) to make a perfectly balanced, impeccably garnished drink. There really is no right or wrong entry level for making great drinks at home—anyone can do it. At the end of the day, at-home bartending isn't so different from cooking. It's all about being inventive with the fresh ingredients you have on hand and keeping an open mind toward experimentation.

I still remember the moment it all clicked for me. I was in my early twenties, and my uncle Brad invited me over for a mini bartending lesson. Knowing that I was starting to take a budding interest in cocktails, Brad cleared off his kitchen island to set up two identical bartending stations, one for me, one for him. Each was equipped with ingredients, shakers, and recipes for three classic cocktails: the old-fashioned, the Aviation, and the sidecar.

With the first sip of my homemade sidecar, I knew this was only the beginning for me. With just three ingredients and some shaking and straining,

I had made a drinkable piece of art—something that would have cost upwards of $15 at a bar but can cost an estimated $4 per drink at home.

Since then, I've made hundreds (maybe thousands) of drinks for friends, family, and the passionate community of Internet cocktail folks who know me as @join_jules online. My uncle Brad and I even host a podcast called *The Art of Drinking*, where Brad takes on a classic every week and I add a modern twist.

My recipes focus on approachability and fresh flavors. You don't need professional experience behind the bar to make an herbaceous, floral masterpiece that channels the smells and sights of walking through a garden.

As someone who grew up in a family that's been farming in Northern California for more than 150 years, I draw a lot of inspiration from the seasons. I like to peruse the farmers' markets and grocery stores in San Diego, where I live, and explore seasonal flavor combinations from what I see there.

As you'll learn from the juices, syrups, and shrubs in this book, there are endless ways to preserve at-peak produce to bring more life into your cocktails.

Whatever you have growing in your garden or ripening on your counter, I hope that reading this book will help you create the happiest of happy hours in the comfort of your own home and empower you to improvise when inspiration strikes.

Make a cocktail right the first time so you know what good tastes like. From there, all that matters is what you like. Like it sweeter? Add a little extra syrup. More tart? Use the whole lime. With a little kick? Add salt to the rim. So, let's grab a glass from the shelf, throw some ice in that shaker, and find you the perfect drink.

How to Think (and Drink) Seasonally

I believe that drinks taste best (and look most beautiful) when they take cues from the seasons.

This means squeezing that full range of bright, floral, bitter flavor from that late-winter citrus harvest, and using peaches when they're at their juiciest, sweetest, end-of-summer best.

Taking inspiration from my local farmers' market and grocery store produce aisle helps me decide what ingredients are at their best, but it can also be helpful to pick a cocktail that fits the mood of the occasion at hand.

I also offer plenty of ways to extend the life of fleeting fruits (persimmons! rhubarb! apricots!) like packing cut fruit into zip-seal bags and freezing for the coming months. You'll also find techniques here for juicing fruit and vegetables without any fancy machines. Or take seasonal ingredients and infuse them into flavored simple syrups, which will last about 4 weeks in the fridge.

Here's a cheat sheet of flavor inspiration for each of the seasons.

SPRING
Apricots, carrots, rhubarb, strawberries

→ **Try a:** Apricot French 75 (page 103), Carrot Margarita (page 86), Rhubarb & Cognac Fizz (page 40), or strawberry-infused Coconut Aperol Margarita (page 81)

SUMMER
Cantaloupe, cherries, nectarines, watermelons

→ **Try a:** Melon No-jito (page 151) or Spicy Watermelon Punch (page 55)

FALL
Apples, cranberries, pumpkin, persimmons

→ **Try a:** Pumpkin-Spiced Irish Coffee (page 126) or Persimmon Mezcal Sour (page 115)

WINTER
Grapefruit, kumquats, lemons, pomegranates

→ **Try a:** The Paloma-rita Sour (page 90), Kumquat Kick (page 52), or Winter Spice Sangria (page 120)

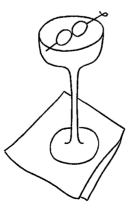

10

The Elements of a Great Cocktail

These are the three elements I think about when making a great cocktail.

Flavor: Set yourself up for success by starting with great ingredients. This means thinking fresh, shopping seasonally, and tasting every single ingredient before adding it to your drink.

Balance: In an ideal cocktail, every flavor component—whether sweet, bitter, acidic, fruity, or floral—plays off the other elements. If you've balanced a drink correctly, it will transcend the sum of its parts. Sometimes this just means following the "bartenders' ratio," an oft-repeated formula of 2 parts spirit, 1 part sour, and 1 part sweet, and sometimes it means tasting as you go and using your instincts to adjust.

Presentation: It's really our eyes that get the first taste—from the glass you choose to serve it in, the ice you scoop into that glass, or the orange twist you garnish it with—it all plays a part in presentation. Take the time to think about these details. You deserve it!

Updates on Classics to Try

→ If you like an **old-fashioned or manhattan,** try the La Dolce Vita on page 125.

→ If you like a **martini,** try the Bianco Spritz on page 69.

→ If you like a **sidecar,** try the Rhubarb & Cognac Fizz on page 40.

→ If you like a **Negroni,** try the Winter Sbagliato on page 66.

→ If you like a **Last Word,** try The Vacationer's Last Word on page 116.

→ If you like a **mint julep,** try the Bourbon & Basil Smash on page 39.

→ If you like a **Paper Plane,** try The Apple-rol Spritz on page 65.

How to Get Started

Even the most inventive cocktails out there usually pay homage to a previous generation's template, and many classic cocktails are really just slight edits to other classic cocktails. You can use these templates to help navigate balance when you're experimenting with your own bar ingredients.

12

A FEW COCKTAIL CATEGORIES TO KNOW

SOUR (THE BARTENDER'S RATIO):

Spirit	+	Sour	+	Sweet
2 parts Spirit		1 part sour		1 part sweet

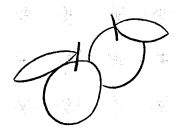

ANCESTRAL (OR "THE OG'S"):

Old-fashioned, Sazerac

Spirit + Sugar + Bitters + Ice (dilution)

OLD-FASHIONED EXAMPLE

2 parts spirit	1/2 part sugar	dashes of bitters	Ice (for stirring)

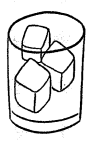

SPIRIT-FORWARD:

Martini, Negroni, manhattan

Spirit + Vermouth or Liqueurs + Bitters + Ice (dilution)

CLASSIC MARTINI

3 parts spirit	1 part dry vermouth	dashes of bitters	Ice (for stirring or shaking)

HIGHBALL:

Whiskey highball, Americano, gin and tonic, paloma

Spirit + nonalcoholic Mixer

2 parts spirit	4 parts nonalcoholic mixer

Your dream bar of essential bottles might look totally different from my dream bar, and that's okay.

Here's my best advice when stocking your home bar: Hold off on buying the *really* expensive top-shelf bottles—at least until you know what you like--and avoid buying the cheapest bottles as well (they usually aren't a great representation of the category of spirit that you're trying). Taste as you go, take notes on what you like, and make sure you're only putting spirits into your cocktails that taste good on their own.

Vodka

There's a common misconception that vodka has no flavor. I beg to differ, and if you taste a handle of the cheap stuff back-to-back with a deliciously clean, crisp vodka, you'll see what I mean. While there are a lot of flavored vodkas on the market, I prefer to buy a really great bottle of the unflavored stuff and infuse it myself.

BOTTLES TO TRY

→ Kástra Elión vodka (perfect for the Olive Oil Martini, page 100)

→ Reyka vodka

→ Grey Goose vodka

Tequila and Mezcal

Fun fact: All tequila is Mezcal but not all Mezcal is tequila. Tequila is made from the blue Weber agave plant, and mezcal (tequila's smoky cousin) can be made from multiple varieties of agave.

The three most common types of tequila are blanco, reposado, and añejo. Blanco is bottled immediately after distillation, reposado is aged in oak barrels for anywhere from 2 to 12 months, and anejo is aged in oak barrels for anywhere from 1 to 3 years.

I like to use blanco when I'm looking for a cleaner, more neutral taste, and an aged tequila in booze-forward drinks when I want to taste a deeper flavor with more honey and caramel notes. Be sure to read the label: if the bottle does not say 100% blue agave, it is a mixto, which can include other types of sugars.

What makes mezcal different is first the variety of the agave used, but mainly it's the slow process used to cook the agave. They are traditionally cooked underground for days, and this is what gives mezcal its unique smoky flavor.

BOTTLES TO TRY

→ El Tesoro blanco tequila

→ Partida reposado tequila

→ Agua Magica mezcal

→ Tequila Ocho Anejo

Gin

Like vodka, gin is crafted as a neutral grain spirit. To be categorized as a gin, it must be made with juniper berries, but it can be flavored with all kinds of herbs and flowers. Some popular styles include London dry, which is juniper- and citrus-forward, and is best for a gin and tonic; and Plymouth-style, which is slightly earthier and drier than the London dry is my favorite for a martini. You'll also see contemporary-style nontraditional gins with flavors that can range from citrus forward to floral—though, to qualify as gin, juniper must always be present.

BOTTLES TO TRY

→ Hendrick's gin (contemporary-style notes of cucumber and rose)

→ Gray Whale gin (notes of mint and pine with a slight sweetness)

→ Plymouth Gin original strength (Plymouth-style notes of angelica root and citrus)

Whiskey

Whiskey is a *category* that includes whiskey, bourbon, Scotch, and rye. They can range in flavor from caramelly and round to peppery and smoky. As you'll learn, I'm partial to the sweet honey notes of bourbon, especially in summery drinks. A common question in the whiskey category (or any spirits category) is the question of pricing. There are many reasons that impact cost, such as where it's made, the quality of ingredients used to make or age the spirit, the length of time the spirit is aged, and the raw materials used to make the spirit—though good marketing and demand comes into play, too.

Bourbon: This spirit needs to be made from at least 51% corn and produced in America. The maturation process must take place in a new oak barrel but has no minimum aging period. Bourbon can be sweeter than other whiskeys, with flavors of vanilla, caramel, and oak. It's my favorite for a whiskey sour.

Scotch: Must be distilled, matured, and bottled in Scotland. The maturation process must occur in an oak barrel for at least 3 years. Generally, Scotch is made from malted barley and can have a smoky character from peat, but it can have a nonsmoky, unpeated flavor as well. It will also have flavors of apples, vanilla, and spices.

Irish whiskey: Must be distilled and matured in Ireland, in wooden casks, for at least 3 years. Irish whiskey has a floral, sweet flavor profile with notes of orchard fruits.

Rye whiskey: This spirit is made in America and must be made from at least 51% rye. Rye has a more spice-forward flavor of cloves and black pepper.

BOTTLES TO TRY

→ Elijah Craig bourbon

→ Glenfiddich single malt Scotch whiskey

→ Tullamore D.E.W. Irish whiskey

→ Angel's Envy rye whiskey

Brandy and Cognac

Every bottle of Cognac is a brandy, but not all brandy is Cognac. Brandy is made from fermented fruit juices, which is why you'll sometimes see bottles labeled specifically as apple brandy or peach brandy. The most popular category is Cognac, which must be made from grapes in the Cognac region of France and aged for at least 2 years in oak barrels. Cognac is great to sip on its own and, of course, great to try in drinks like the Rhubarb & Cognac Fizz (page 40).

BOTTLES TO TRY

→ Rémy Martin 1738 Accord Royal

→ Cognac de Luze VS

→ Laird's Straight Applejack 86 apple brandy

Rum

Rum, which is distilled from molasses or sugarcane, can be found in a whole spectrum of colors based on how the spirit has been aged. I recommend starting with one white or light rum, which you'll use in drinks like mojitos and daiquiris, and one dark rum, which will come into play in tropical drinks or as a stand-in for whiskey in some old-fashioned recipes.

BOTTLES TO TRY

→ Ten to One Caribbean white rum

→ Appleton Estate Signature Jamaica rum

→ Plantation Original Dark rum

Bitter Liqueurs

Amaro means "bitter" in Italian, and it ranges from the sweet-bitter flavors of the popular Aperol to the warm bittersweet flavors of Cynar (an artichoke amaro). The difference between an aperitif and a digestif is that aperitifs are to be enjoyed before a meal to stimulate one's appetite, and they are typically drier with slight sweetness. On the other hand, a digestif is served after a meal to aid digestion; they are typically higher in alcohol and tend to have a bitter profile.

BOTTLES TO TRY

→ Campari or try Contratto bitter

→ Aperol or try Cappalletti Aperitivo

→ Amaro Nonino (for a Paper Plane cocktail)

→ Italicus Rosolio di Bergamotto (made with Calabrian bergamot citrus fruit)

Vermouth

It wouldn't be a martini without a splash of dry vermouth, or a Negroni without a pour of sweet vermouth. Dry vermouth is the color of white wine, and it contains about 5% sugar. Sweet vermouth, which has an amber-maroon color, contains closer to 15% sugar (hence the name) and can sometimes contain warm spice notes, like vanilla or cinnamon. Sweet vermouth isn't going to be sweet like a liqueur, but it will be sweeter than dry vermouth. Since vermouth is a fortified wine, with a relatively low alcohol percentage, it can deteriorate over time, so keep your bottle in the fridge once it's opened and try to use it up within a few weeks.

Here's a good rule of thumb to remember: If it's under 15% ABV or is wine-based (like Lillet), it should be stored in the fridge after opening.

BOTTLES TO TRY

→ Lo-Fi Aperitifs dry vermouth

→ Dolin dry vermouth

→ Cocchi Vermouth di Torino

Bubbles

Whether you're making a gin and tonic or an Aperol Spritz, you're gonna need some bubbles. Those bubbles can take the form of club soda, sparkling water (seltzer), tonic water, or sparkling wine. Club soda has both minerals and carbonation added, which comes in handy when you want big, vivacious bubbles without bringing in any additional sweetness or alcohol. Sparkling water (or seltzer/mineral water) is naturally carbonated water with natural minerals retained; therefore, the bubbles and flavor can vary by brand. If you'll frequent the spritz chapter, a sparkling water maker like SodaStream is a worthy investment. With its slight bitter sweetness, tonic water is a perfect pairing for botanical gin, but it can also add dimension to nonalcoholic cocktails. Sparkling wine is key in many spritzes and punches in this book.

I often recommend prosecco when I'm looking for something sweet and fruity. I also like Cava or Champagne when I'm looking for something dry and crisp.

BOTTLES TO TRY

→ Cinzano prosecco

→ Billecart-Salmon Champagne

→ Fever-Tree tonics

→ Jarritos Mineragua sparkling water

Flavored Liqueurs

In addition to all the standard base spirits we've already covered, there's a whole world out there of flavored liqueurs just waiting to fine-tune your drink with just the right amount of orange-peel essence, almond nuttiness, or earthy gentian root. As a margarita fanatic, I always have plenty of orange liqueur (like Cointreau) around, plus some orange Curaçao for tropical drinks. But here are some other liqueurs we'll be using throughout this book!

BOTTLES TO TRY

→ Ancho Reyes ancho chile liqueur

→ Chinola passion fruit liqueur

→ Green Chartreuse

→ St-Germain elderflower liqueur

→ Licor 43

Cocktail Shaker

You need a cocktail shaker when making a drink that calls for fresh juices, cream, or eggs.

Cocktail shakers shake, aerate, and dilute your cocktail while chilling all those ingredients at the same time. Shaking can help create a froth and also aerate the liquid, which changes the cocktail's texture.

In a pinch? Use any container that seals tightly, like a mason jar, protein shaker bottle, or airtight travel coffee mug.

Mixing Glass

A sturdy, thick-walled, spouted mixing glass is perfectly designed for stirring cocktails that are spirit-forward and don't have juices added to them. This helps quickly cool down drinks like an old-fashioned, without diluting them too much. It's a good rule of thumb to stir for about 20 seconds to allow the ice to melt slightly, giving the proper dilution.

In a pinch? You just need a glass that is larger than your serving glass; try a pint glass, a French-press container, or a 2-cup liquid measuring cup of your choice.

Jigger

A jigger is a bar measuring tool that makes it easy to tip precise measurements of spirits, syrups, and juices into a cocktail. Some are double-sided, with each side accommodating a different amount of liquid.

In a pinch? Pull out the liquid measuring cups and spoons and check out the handy Conversion Cheat Sheet (page 20).

Strainer

Straining a drink over fresh ice (or into a chilled glass without ice in some cases) gives the drink a consistent, clear texture and refined presentation. Hawthorne strainers help eliminate ice and muddled ingredients, julep strainers are designed to hold back the ice in a mixing glass, and a fine-mesh sieve helps keep little bits of fruit pulp and tiny shards of ice out of the final serving glass.

In a pinch? Use a slotted spoon or a mason jar lid to try to hold back the ice, and if you want to double-strain, pair this method with a fine-mesh sieve or a tea strainer.

Citrus Juicer

If it's not fresh, we don't want it! That's why I like to keep a hinged citrus juicer or handheld reamer at the ready for when I'm making cocktails.

In a pinch? Roll the whole citrus on a hard surface with pressure to release the juices. Next, cut the citrus in half and rotate a fork around the pulp to draw out the juice. You can always strain it through your fingers to catch any seeds.

Muddler

A muddler looks a bit like a pestle, and it's used to lightly mash fruits, herbs, or spices for your cocktail—either in a pint glass, a rocks glass, or a shaker. The best way to use a muddler is to press it.

In a pinch? If you don't have a muddler, use the blunt end of a wooden spoon.

Barspoon

A barspoon is a narrow long-handled spoon that's used to stir cocktails, sometimes to carefully layer liquid ingredients in the glass for a dramatic visual effect.

In a pinch? Use a straw (especially a sturdy metal straw) or a chopstick to stir your cocktail.

Peelers and Zesters

For cutting perfect ribbons of citrus peel to garnish a cocktail, nothing gets the job done like a sharp Y-shaped peeler. And for grating citrus zest into perfect, aromatic strands of confetti, or for gently shaving a sprinkle of fresh nutmeg over a drink, I always keep a sharp zester or Microplane near.

In a pinch? Use a sharp paring knife to make a citrus peel. Just cut slowly and carefully while rotating the fruit. And for grating zest, try a cheese grater!

Blender

A high-powered blender is key for making frozen cocktails and slushies a breeze, turning ice cubes into crushed ice, or creating juices and purees.

In a pinch? Try a food processor or immersion blender. If you don't mind putting a little elbow grease into the process, you can also muddle and then strain your way to fresh juice.

Hand Frother

I like to use it to make flavored creams for topping sweeter drinks and to aerate egg whites for frothy cocktails.

In a pinch? Use an electric hand mixer or cocktail shaker to whip cream and aerate your egg whites.

Kitchen Torch

Having one of these inexpensive butane torches on hand means that you're only ever a couple minutes away from a perfectly brûléed lemon wheel to top your Lemon Meringue Martini (page 134) or from bathing your cocktail glass with rosemary-scented smoke.

In a pinch? Without a torch, you can brûlé fruit garnishes on a sheet pan under the broiler or (carefully!) ignite garnishes like the rosemary using a lighter or a match.

CONVERSION CHEAT SHEET

1 dash = 1 milliliter

⅛ ounce = 1 teaspoon = 4 milliliters

½ ounce = 3 teaspoons = 1 tablespoon = 15 milliliters

¾ ounce = 1·½ tablespoons = 22 milliliters

1 ounce = 2 tablespoons = 30 milliliters

1·½ ounces = 3 tablespoons = 45 milliliters

2 ounces = 4 tablespoons = ¼ cup = 60 milliliters

3 ounces = ¼ cup + 2 tablespoons = 90 milliliters

4 ounces = ½ cup = 120 milliliters

5 ounces = ½ cup + 2 tablespoons = 150 milliliters

6 ounces = ¾ cup = 180 milliliters

7 ounces = ¾ cup + 2 tablespoons = 210 milliliters

8 ounces = 1 cup = 240 milliliters

12 ounces = 1·½ cups = 360 milliliters

1 large kitchen spoon (soup spoon) = ½ ounce

1 coffee spoon (demitasse spoon) = ⅛ ounce or a splash

Average shot glass = 1·½ ounces

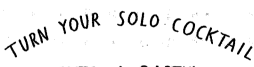

TURN YOUR SOLO COCKTAIL
INTO A PARTY!

Batch any cocktail into 8 servings by converting ounces
to cups. Example: 1 ounce of vodka becomes 1 cup;
½ ounce of simple syrup becomes ½ cup.
Slight tweaking may be needed, but this is a great
starting point — remember to taste as you go!

My Three Must-Have Glasses

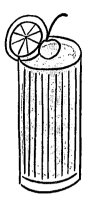

COUPES

These stemmed glasses are by far my favorite glassware to use. Coupes have wide, shallow cups that are perfect for anything shaken or stirred and served up. They usually hold between 4 and 6 ounces, so these are great for boozier, smaller drinks like martinis and daiquiris and Champagne.

HIGHBALLS

Slender, cylindrical glasses that hold 8 to 12 ounces, making them just right for bubbly, refreshing iced drinks like gin and tonics, Palomas, Dark 'n Stormys, and mojitos. There's usually plenty of room to build the drink right in the glass, top it with the tonic or club soda of your choice, and give it a swizzle with your favorite sleek straw.

ROCKS

Squat, stemless glasses that hold between 6 and 8 ounces and is usually wide enough to fit a big ice cube. They're also useful for frozen or blended drinks, or even wine if your party has run out of stemmed wine glasses. A "double rocks glass" or "double old-fashioned glass" will hold up to 12 ounces.

22

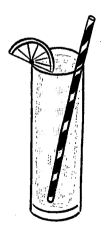

CHAMPAGNE FLUTE
This tall, narrow, stemmed glass holds approximately 6 to 7 ounces. It is an elegant way to serve Champagne or Champagne-based cocktails, like mimosas, Bellinis, or French 75s.

COFFEE GLASS
For hot drinks (like the Après Ski Hot Chocolate, page 130, or the Pumpkin-Spiced Irish Coffee, page 126), it's a good idea to use a thick-walled, sturdy glass with a handle or stem to hold onto. Look for Irish coffee mugs or Georgian glasses that hold 8 to 9 ounces for these drinks.

COLLINS GLASS
Think of this as a slightly taller, slenderer version of the highball glass. Holding about 12 ounces, this glass is perfect for those classic cocktails like a mojito or Tom Collins.

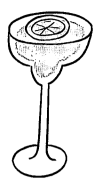

MARGARITA GLASS
If you're a margarita fanatic like me, consider picking up a few of these rocks, stemmed, or traditional margarita glasses to bring a vacation mindset to your home bar.

MARTINI GLASS
A classic V-shaped martini glass that holds about 6 ounces can give the presentation some twentieth-century drama and glamor.

NICK & NORA GLASS
This stemmed glass has a petite, tulip-shaped cup holding about 4 ounces. It's a great alternative to the coupe.

WINE GLASS
Larger wine glasses are perfect for spritzes, and a stemless wine glass can serve as great rocks glass.

I know from experience that it's easy to skimp on ice (especially when your tray is down to the last few cubes), but a mixing glass should be filled with enough ice so that the ice rises about 1 inch above the liquid added. If you're shaking, make sure that there's enough ice in the mixing glass so that you can hear the ice hitting each end of it as you shake that drink. When hosting a crowd, it's also important to make plenty of ice ahead of time and store it in freezer bags to ensure you don't run out!

To keep drinks colder for longer and to keep the ice in your serving glass from turning into a puddle too soon, it always helps to chill your glass. As soon as you know what drink you're making, just stick your glass of choice upright in the freezer. If you forget to chill your serving glass ahead of time, you can also speed up the process by filling it with ice and water while you make your drink and dumping the ice water out just before filling the glass with your drink.

The Types of Ice You'll See Most Frequently in This Book

STANDARD ICE CUBES

On almost every page of this book, you'll see me calling for standard ice cubes to help shake, stir, or serve a drink. When I say "standard," I just mean the regular ice cubes (usually around 1 inch by 1 inch).

LARGE ICE CUBES

Many houseware stores sell silicone ice cube trays that make 2-inch cubes—the size that I refer to as "large" throughout this book. They melt slowly, allowing you to sip at a leisurely pace. I also like to throw one larger ice cube in with a scoop of standard ice cubes to shake frothy drinks. I find that it creates a great texture of foam.

CRACKED ICE

Cracked ice falls somewhere between standard ice cubes and crushed ice. You can make it by using the back of a barspoon (and brute force) to whack apart a few large ice cubes. When making freshly cracked ice, it exposes the cold center of the ice, which is perfect for quick cooling when stirring booze-forward drinks.

How to Elevate Your Ice

THINK OUTSIDE THE CUBE

While standard ice cubes are space-efficient for packed freezers and get the job done, there's a whole world out there of cool ice molds to experiment with. The best way to impress your guests is taking the extra step to create clear ice. The easiest way to do this is with a clear ice mold device! If you're tired of trying to fit ice cubes awkwardly into your collins glass, get a collins ice cube tray, which produces long, slender cubes. These are only the beginning—you can find molds to shape your ice into gems, flowers, animals, and just about any novelty item your heart desires (including hearts).

ADD SOME FLAIR

Suspending garnishes inside ice cubes is an unexpected but extremely easy way to make your drink even more impressive. You can add flower petals, fruit slices, or fresh herb leaves to each cube of water before it freezes.

A Guide to Garnishing

A Rimmed Glass

One of the easiest ways to garnish cocktails is by rimming the glass, and a margarita is just the beginning. You can rim a glass with sugar, chile-lime seasoning like Tajín, and even crushed candy (peppermint sticks). All you need is a liquid to wet the glass (lime juice, chocolate syrup, honey, simple syrup) and a powdered or granulated mixture of some kind to adhere to the rim.

Prepare two small plates or saucers (just slightly wider than the glass you're using): one for the wet component and one for the dry. Twist just the outside rim in the liquid (or rub a cut lime around the rim) and then hold it upside down for a few seconds to air-dry it slightly and allow any excess moisture to drip off. Next, gently roll the outside rim in the dry ingredient (rim only the outside rim, as this will keep the salt from falling into the drink and changing the flavor). Pop that whole glass in the freezer to help halt drips and chill your glass at the same time.

A Frosted Glass

So elegant. Just fill a mister or atomizer with simple syrup or citrus juice, spray the outside of the glass near the rim and around one side of the glass, and use a fine-mesh sieve to gently dust the moist part of the glass with a powdered ingredient (do this over a bowl to catch any that doesn't adhere). If you don't have an atomizer, you can also very lightly brush the glass using a pastry brush. You can use finely ground salt, white granulated sugar, matcha, cocoa powder, or even dehydrated fruit (like strawberry or mango) that has been pulverized to a powder in a blender. This will give your glass a frosted window look.

Do the Twist or Swath

A **twist** expresses the oils and aromatics of the citrus onto your drink and around the lip of your glass. Using a Y-peeler (or paring knife), pull a wide strip of zest from citrus and use a knife to trim the peel so both sides are straight. Twist the peel around a barspoon or toothpick and squeeze slightly to help it hold its shape. Remove from the barspoon and lean it up against the side of the glass or perch it on the rim.

A **swath** expresses fresh citrus oils without the twist. Using a Y-peeler (or paring knife) to pull a wide strip of zest from the citrus. Squeeze the zest strip skin-side out over the drink and wipe it around the rim of the glass, then drop the peel right into the glass for a little garnish option.

Wheels and Wedges

This is as simple as cutting the citrus crosswise into thin, round slices using a sharp knife and adding the wheel to the inside of the glass or perching it on the rim by cutting a slit halfway through. To cut a piece of fruit into wedges, just cut it in half crosswise, and divide each half into thirds.

28

Dehydrate Those Slices

Dehydrated wheels are a practical way to extend the shelf life of that fruit.

To dehydrate citrus wheels, preheat the oven to 170°F (or as low as it will go). Set a wire cooling rack into a baking sheet and place ¼-inch-thick wheels on it. Transfer to the oven and bake for 3 to 6 hours, rotating the baking tray and flipping the citrus wheels with tongs every couple of hours. The citrus wheels are done once they feel completely light and dry. Remove them from the oven and allow them to cool to room temperature, then store in an airtight container for up to 6 months.

To make dehydrated pineapple flower wheels, preheat the oven to 225°F. Take a fresh pineapple and cut off the top and bottom and carefully remove the skin. Set a wire cooling rack into a baking sheet and slice and place ¼-inch-thick pineapple rounds on it. Transfer the baking sheet to the oven and bake for 30 minutes, until the tops look dried, then flip the slices and cook again for another 25 minutes until completely dried. Remove them from the oven and allow them to cool to room temperature, then store in an airtight container for up to 6 months.

Give Fruit the Brûlée Treatment

If you have a kitchen torch (and you totally should), you're just a few seconds away from adding a layer of burnt-sugar complexity to your next fruit garnish. Pat dry fresh-cut fruit, such as an orange slice or piece of banana, and sprinkle some granulated sugar across the cut side. Toast the sugar with the torch until it starts to bubble and turn the color of caramel.

Get Fired Up

Flaming cocktails are easier than you think, as long as you proceed with caution and make sure you have cleared your surroundings of flammable objects (for real, no joke). Here are some quick and easy ways to create a flaming garnish.

Overproof rum and a sugar cube: Start with a juiced lime half and set it squeezed-side up (to create a small bowl shape) on top of the ice of the cocktail (see the Kentucky Jungle Bird, page 107). Place a sugar cube in the middle of the lime "bowl" and add a few drops (about ¼ ounce) of 151 overproof rum on top. Use a kitchen torch, lighter, or match to ignite the 151-doused sugar cube. Once the cube is lit, hold a fine-mesh sieve filled with ground cinnamon safely above the sugar cube and sprinkle the cinnamon over the lime for dramatic flames. Before drinking, make sure to blow out the flame or wait until it's extinguished.

Citrus zest: Use a Y-peeler to cut a fresh strip of citrus zest. Gently grab the citrus zest and point the skin side toward the drink. It's best practice to hold the peel about 5 inches from the cocktail with your nondominant hand

and ignite a match with the dominant hand. Once you have everything ready, light the match and place it directly next to the surface of the outer peel. Pinch the peel to curl it toward the flame, which will express its oils, igniting a momentary flame and add some smoky, caramelized notes to the citrus oils. Use the peel as a garnish by dropping it straight into your cocktail or discard it.

Get Graphic with Bitters

Yes, bitters are an integral ingredient in many cocktails, but they can also be used as a garnish, especially if your drink has a fluffy layer of egg white froth on top. Create a heart pattern by dropping a row of side-by-side dots across the surface of the drink. Use a toothpick to drag through the middle of each dot to join the pairs together in little heart shapes. Or dot the surface with three or four drops of bitters and drag a toothpick through them into a freeform swirl pattern.

Edible Flowers

Edible flowers are a pretty way to garnish cocktails and an easy way to upgrade ice, and they can even be used in simple syrup recipes. When purchasing, make sure the flowers are labeled as edible and have not been treated with any pesticides or chemicals. Many grocery stores, like Whole Foods and Trader Joe's, sell edible flowers in the produce section, and you can also shop online from websites like Gourmet Sweet

Botanicals, Marx Foods, and Melissa's Produce. Here are a few favorites:

- → Anise hyssop
- → Bee balm
- → Borage
- → Buzz buttons
- → Calendula
- → Chamomile
- → Daylily
- → Fennel
- → Hibiscus
- → Honeysuckle
- → Lavender
- → Marigolds
- → Mint
- → Nasturtiums
- → Pansies
- → Parsley
- → Rose
- → Rosemary
- → Sage
- → Squash blossoms
- → Thyme
- → Violas
- → Violet

Turn Seasonal Produce into Garnishes!

Berries: Skewer three onto a cocktail pick.

Apples and pears: Add a stack of fanned slices to a cocktail pick.

Pomegranate seeds: Add these directly to the drink or freeze in ice cubes.

Cucumbers, rhubarb, carrots: Use a Y-peeler to cut ribbons to twist around the inside of the glass.

Pineapple leaves: Gently pull the leaves off the top of a pineapple and use as a garnish. You can always pull the leaves off the top of a pineapple, place in a zip-seal bag, and freeze for future use.

Relaxed
Refreshers

This chapter is dedicated to the refreshing, breezy, light drinks I turn to when I'm enjoying a leisurely brunch or catching up with friends during a weekend afternoon by the pool. Often lower-ABV (like the seasonal Lillet Highball, page 51) and even alcohol-free (like The Verde Maria, page 35), these are the coolers, fizzes, and daiquiris, full of rejuvenating, seasonal ingredients, that you'll want to tap for session drinking and daytime parties.

the
verde maria

I thought it was about time to give everyone's favorite brunch cocktail, the Bloody Mary, a verdant makeover, so I swapped the tomatoes for a refreshing blend of tomatillos and cucumbers, and the usual vodka for tequila, which complements the spice and citrus. Even if you skip the alcohol altogether, this hydrating, herbaceous, and peppery cocktail will get your day going.

For the rim: lime wedge and celery salt

Standard ice cubes

6 ounces Verde Maria Mix (recipe follows)

2 ounces tequila blanco (or vodka)

Garnishes: Celery stalk, pickles, cherry tomatoes, crispy-cooked bacon

Verde Maria Mix

2 Persian (mini) cucumbers, roughly chopped

8 tomatillos (see Tip), husked, rinsed, and halved

1 jalapeño, halved (seeded for a less spicy mix)

½ bunch parsley, stems removed

2 ounces pickle juice

1 ounce fresh lemon juice

1 ounce fresh lime juice

1 ounce green Tabasco sauce

1 tablespoon horseradish

½ teaspoon celery salt

½ teaspoon freshly ground black pepper

Run a lime wedge around the rim of a collins glass and roll the rim in celery salt (see A Rimmed Glass, page 28). Fill the glass about halfway with ice, to save room to garnish.

In an ice-filled cocktail shaker, combine the Verde Maria mix and tequila. Cover and shake vigorously for 30 seconds. Strain into the prepared glass and garnish with celery, pickles, cherry tomatoes, and/or a slice of bacon.

Verde Maria Mix

MAKES 3½ CUPS (28 OUNCES) /
ENOUGH FOR 4 COCKTAILS

In a blender, combine the cucumbers, tomatillos, jalapeño, parsley, pickle juice, lemon and lime juices, Tabasco sauce, horseradish, celery salt, and black pepper and blend until smooth. Strain and chill for at least 2 hours before using.

FOR A SMOKY EDGE
Cook whole husked tomatillos for about 20 minutes in a cast-iron skillet over medium heat, rotating occasionally, until they start to char and begin to soften. Husk, halve, and use in place of raw tomatillos.

breakfast of champions

This brunch-friendly drink, which I've been making for years, gets its soft, foamy texture from a tiny bit of Greek yogurt and a touch of bubbly tonic water. Yogurt in a cocktail might sound strange if you've never had it, but trust me—it adds a richness and a tang that balances beautifully between the herbaceous gin and the fruity strawberry syrup. Think of this as your morning bowl of fruit and yogurt, translated into cocktail form.

2 ounces gin (try Gray Whale gin)

1 heaping teaspoon plain whole-milk Greek yogurt

¾ ounce freshly squeezed lemon juice

½ ounce Strawberry Syrup (page 161)

Standard ice cubes, for shaking and serving

2 ounces tonic water

Mint sprigs, for garnish

Freshly cracked pepper, for garnish (optional)

In a cocktail shaker, combine the gin, yogurt, lemon juice, and strawberry syrup. Add ice, cover, and shake vigorously for 30 seconds. Double-strain into an ice-filled double rocks glass or stemless wine glass. Top with tonic water, "smack the mint" (see Tip), add the sprigs to the glass, crack fresh pepper on top, if using, and serve.

SMACK THE MINT
When garnishing with fresh mint, try taking the sprigs of mint in one hand and smacking the mint gently into the other hand. This will help to express not only the oils but the aromas of the mint, which will take the drink up a notch.

bourbon & basil smash

MAKES 1 COCKTAIL

Think of this as the mint julep's sassy, summery cousin. Fresh basil (and a splash of basil simple syrup) adds a grassy, peppery brightness to the equation, with the lemon keeping each sip puckeringly juicy. Ginger beer brings a warm prickle of spice that makes an unexpected harmonious combination with the basil. Since there are lots of sweet components at play here, pick a ginger beer that veers a little spicier and a little less sweet.

2 ounces bourbon (try Four Roses)

¾ ounce freshly squeezed lemon juice

½ ounce basil simple syrup (see Herbaceous Syrups, page 162)

Standard ice cubes, for shaking

Large ice cube, for serving

1 ounce ginger beer, such as Fever Tree, for topping

Basil sprig, for garnish

Put a rocks glass in the freezer to chill.

In a cocktail shaker, combine the bourbon, lemon juice, and basil syrup. Add ice, cover, and shake vigorously for 30 seconds. Double-strain into the chilled rocks glass over a large ice cube. Top with the ginger beer. Place a fresh sprig of basil on top.

QUICK BASIL SYRUP, ON THE GO
If you're low on basil simple syrup, add ½ ounce simple syrup plus 3 or 4 basil leaves right into your shaker instead!

rhubarb & cognac fizz

MAKES 1 COCKTAIL

This cocktail is a bit like a slice of strawberry rhubarb pie in a refreshing, fizzy form. Since it combines two different preservation methods (a ruby-red syrup made from strawberries and a rosy shrub made from rhubarb), it's a great way to hang onto those fleeting early-summer flavors a little longer. The homemade rhubarb shrub requires about 5 days of preparation in advance, but once it's done you'll have it at the ready for the weeks (even months) to come. You can turn your farmers' market bounty into these building blocks on a Sunday afternoon and then enjoy several weeks' worth of cocktails. In this drink, the light bubbles and Cognac add a whole new dynamic to that familiar rhubarb flavor—you could also keep it alcohol-free and mix the shrub with some sparkling water and a splash of syrup.

1½ ounces Cognac (try Hine Cognac VSOP)

¾ ounce freshly squeezed lemon juice

¾ ounce orange liqueur

½ ounce Rhubarb Shrub (page 167)

½ ounce Strawberry Syrup (page 161)

Standard ice cubes, for shaking and serving

Fresh rhubarb, for garnish

2 ounces club soda, for topping

In a cocktail shaker, combine the Cognac, lemon juice, orange liqueur, rhubarb shrub, and strawberry syrup. Add ice, cover, and shake vigorously for 30 seconds.

Use a Y-peeler to cut a delicate ribbon of rhubarb and use a pair of tongs to twist it around the interior and exterior of the highball glass.

Double-strain into an ice-filled highball glass. Top with club soda.

40

lemon prosecco pops

MAKES 10 ICE POPS

These boozy, prosecco ice pops are cool and crushable, and you can make them ahead of time to keep your party guests refreshed and relaxed. Straight from the ice pop molds, they are balanced and summery with plenty of zesty lemon flavor. Once you have the hang of the basic ratios, feel free to put your own seasonal spin on these, swapping in blood orange juice for the lemon juice, or 2 cups of a seasonal flavored syrup in place of the classic simple syrup. Want to branch out beyond the prosecco to make your own custom frozen margarita pops or vodka-spiked confection? Experiment with hard spirits by following a ratio of about ½ ounce of booze to 2½ ounces of syrup and juice per pop (to ensure they freeze). Make things even more festive and serve the pops inverted into glasses of prosecco!

Special tools: 10 (3-ounce) ice pop molds (see Tip)

¼ cup granulated sugar

2 cups water

2 cups prosecco, plus more for serving (try La Marca Prosecco)

Grated zest of 1 lemon

⅓ cup (or 2½ ounces) freshly squeezed lemon juice (about 3 large lemons)

10 mint sprigs

In a medium saucepan, combine the sugar and water and stir over medium heat until the sugar fully dissolves. Set aside at room temperature to allow the syrup to cool completely.

In a big mixing glass or pitcher, stir together the cooled syrup, prosecco, lemon zest, and lemon juice. Divide the mixture among ten 3-ounce ice pop molds. Place a mint sprig in each mold.

Freeze for at least 4 hours or until solid. Pop out and serve.

DON'T HAVE ICE POP MOLDS?
Freeze these in ice cube trays and use the resulting cubes to chill your next glass of prosecco.

jules's piña colada

MAKES 1 COCKTAIL

When done right, this tropical cocktail has the power to wash your cares away (whether you're caught in the rain or not). While a lot of versions you'll find in dive-y beach bars can be overly sweet and headache-inducing, my ideal colada is balanced and bright. The key is to use fresh pineapple juice, fresh lime juice, and skip the cream of coconut in favor of coconut cream. While these similarly named ingredients are easy to confuse, cream of coconut can be packed with added sugar, while coconut cream provides pure coconut flavor and richness without any added sweetness (making it easy to customize the drink to your preferred sweetness).

1½ ounces white rum
  (try Plantation 3 Stars)

1 ounce aged rum
  (try Smith & Cross)

1½ ounces Fresh Pineapple Juice
  (page 82)

1 tablespoon coconut cream
  (or the cream layer skimmed
  off a can of coconut milk)

½ ounce Plain Simple Syrup
  (page 160)

½ ounce freshly squeezed lime juice

Standard ice cubes, for shaking
  and serving

1 whole nutmeg, for grating

Pineapple leaves, for garnish

Fish tacos, for serving (optional
  and *highly* recommended)

Place a medium stemmed glass or highball glass in the freezer to chill.

In a cocktail shaker, combine the white rum, aged rum, pineapple juice, coconut cream, simple syrup, and lime juice. Add ice cubes, cover, and shake vigorously for 30 seconds. Strain into the preferred chilled glass filled with ice.

Grate fresh nutmeg over the top and tuck a few pineapple leaves into the glass.

CUSTOMIZE YOUR COLADA
Turn up the sweetness by adding ¼ ounce Plain Simple Syrup (page 160) for a total of ¾ ounce syrup. To turn this into a frozen piña colada, just add the ingredients to a blender with 1 cup of ice and blend on medium-high speed until smooth.

44

the
pink daiquiri

MAKES 1 COCKTAIL

I first made this drink with ingredients lying around my kitchen, and it's held a high ranking in my cocktail repertoire ever since. I took the structure of a classic daiquiri (rum, lime juice, and sugar), swapped some strawberry syrup in for the sweetener, and added a splash of coconut milk for a creamy consistency. After giving it a shake, it took on a dreamy pale-pink hue, and I've been making it ever since. This is a great back-pocket cocktail to remember when you have those occasional splashes of coconut milk left over in the refrigerator. If you happen to have some good strawberries on hand, you can skewer two halves together on a cocktail pick to look like a little heart.

2 ounces light rum
(try Lafcadio Botanical Rum)

1 ounce canned unsweetened coconut milk (try Thai Kitchen)

¾ ounce freshly squeezed lime juice

½ ounce Strawberry Syrup (page 161)

Standard ice cubes, for shaking

Dehydrated lime wheel (see Dehydrate Those Slices, page 29) or skewered strawberry halves, for garnish

Place a coupe glass in the freezer to chill.

In a cocktail shaker, combine the rum, coconut milk, lime juice, and strawberry syrup. Add ice, cover, and shake vigorously for 30 seconds. Double-strain into the chilled coupe glass and garnish with a dehydrated lime wheel or strawberry halves.

frozen peach palmer

Think of this as a peachy, frozen, boozy Arnold Palmer. The flash of black tea adds a gentle tannic edge that perfectly complements the bourbon, honey, and fresh fruit. Make this in late summer, when peaches and nectarines are in season, or freeze them when they are in season to use later.

½ cup frozen peach or nectarine chunks

2 ounces bourbon (try Old Forester)

1 ounce freshly squeezed lemon juice

1 ounce black tea or sun tea, homemade (see Tip) or store-bought

2 teaspoons Honey Syrup (page 160)

1 cup crushed ice, for blending

Fresh lemon wheel, for garnish

Mint sprig, for garnish

Place a rocks glass or stemless wine glass in the freezer to chill.

In a blender, combine the frozen peaches, bourbon, lemon juice, black tea, honey syrup, and 1 cup crushed ice and blend on medium-high speed until smooth and no visible chunks remain, 1 to 2 minutes.

Pour into the chilled glass, garnish with the lemon wheel and a gently slapped fresh mint sprig (see Tip, page 36).

HOMEMADE SUN TEA

Ever take advantage of the summer sun to help with your tea making? Every summer, when the days are long and the sun is hot, my mother makes sun tea. I recently made it with her, and it is easier than you think. Just place 8 black tea bags into a gallon container and fill the gallon jar with water until it reaches the top. Place the lid on top and let sit in the sun all day (or for at least 5 hours in direct sunlight). Remove and discard the tea bags and store the tea in the refrigerator for up to 2 days.

pretty simple cocktails

PHOTOGRAPHS BY LUCIANNA MCINTOSH

 CLARKSON POTTER/PUBLISHERS
NEW YORK

lillet highball

A classic whiskey highball generally follows a formula of about 2 ounces whiskey mixed with about 4 ounces club soda and is served in a tall glass over ice. This highball gets its low-ABV kick of soft, floral sweetness by using Lillet Blanc instead of whiskey as the base spirit. The aperitif has plenty of character to hold its own over ice with club soda, but it also goes beautifully with a whole year's worth of fruit flavors, so this recipe is built to change with the seasons (see Seasonal Highballs, below). If the fruit you're using isn't as easy to juice, just blend 1 cup of the fruit with ½ cup water and strain to make a fresh fruit puree.

1 long clear ice cube or a few clear
   medium ice cubes, for serving

1 ounce Lillet Blanc

1 ounce seasonal and
   fresh fruit juice

4 ounces club soda

Optional garnishes: seasonal fresh
   herbs, edible flowers, and/or fruit

Place the ice in a highball glass. Add the Lillet Blanc, fruit juice, and club soda and stir gently with a barspoon. If desired, garnish with herbs, edible flowers, and/or fruit and serve.

SEASONAL HIGHBALLS

Spring: 1 ounce strawberry or blackberry juice + fresh berries for garnish

Summer: peach or nectarine juice + fresh violas or pansies for garnish

Fall: pomegranate or cranberry juice + fresh thyme or rosemary for garnish

Winter: tart citrus juices, like grapefruit or mandarin orange + a fresh citrus wheel for garnish

kumquat kick

MAKES 1 COCKTAIL

Unlike many members of the citrus family, kumquats are 100 percent edible—even their delicate skins are packed with sweet-tart flavor. In this low-ABV tonic, I muddle kumquat slices with fresh basil leaves and honey syrup. The sour flavor that's drawn out is a perfect match for smoky chile liqueur, fresh orange juice, and a splash of fizzy tonic water. Make this one between late fall and mid-January, when kumquats are easy to spot at the grocery store. And if you feel like even more kick, add a splash of your favorite bourbon or gin.

4 kumquats, thinly sliced crosswise

3 fresh basil leaves

½ ounce Honey Syrup (page 160), Plain Simple Syrup (page 160), or Spicy Pepper Syrup (page 166)

¾ ounce chile liqueur

1 ounce freshly squeezed orange juice

Standard ice cubes, for shaking and serving

4 ounces tonic water or club soda, for topping

Fresh basil leaf, for garnish

Fresh kumquat slice, for garnish

In a cocktail shaker, combine the kumquats, basil leaves, and honey syrup. Use a muddler to muddle the ingredients, then add the chile liqueur and orange juice. Add ice, cover, and shake vigorously for 30 seconds. Double-strain into a double rocks glass filled with ice. Top with tonic water and garnish with a fresh basil leaf and a fresh kumquat slice.

spicy watermelon punch

MAKES 10 COCKTAILS

While plenty of the punches in this book start with a mix of spirits, syrups, and juices, this one starts out with a vibrant and hydrating agua fresca. A whiz in the blender turns juicy watermelon into an easygoing ruby-red base that can be punched up with a squeeze of lime and splash of simple syrup. This means that you can get that sweet-tart balance of watermelon and lime juice perfect to your liking before adding any spirits or spiciness to the punch. Best of all, you can keep it nonalcoholic if you choose.

3 cups cubed seedless watermelon

2 cups cold filtered water

½ cup freshly squeezed lime juice (from about 4 limes)

8 fresh mint leaves

¼ cup Spicy Pepper Syrup (page 166) or Plain Simple Syrup (page 160)

3 to 4 cups standard ice cubes, for the pitcher, plus more for individual glasses

1½ cups vodka (try Reyka)

¼ cup chile liqueur

Sparkling water, such as Jarritos or Topo Chico, for serving

Mint sprigs, for garnish

Fresh lime wheels, for garnish

In a blender, combine the watermelon, water, lime juice, mint leaves, and spicy pepper syrup and blend on medium-high speed until smooth. Strain through a fine-mesh sieve into a pitcher. Place in the fridge until ready to serve. This mixture will last up to 2 days.

When ready to serve, add 3 to 4 cups of ice to the pitcher and stir in the vodka and chile liqueur (or place the bottles to the side so that guests can choose their own strength).

To serve, pour 5 ounces of punch into an ice-filled rocks glass. Top with about 1 ounce of sparkling water. Gently slap a fresh mint sprig (see Tip, page 36) and place it into the glass along with a fresh lime wheel.

LOOKING FOR A NONALCOHOLIC OPTION? Just omit the vodka and chile liqueur. To keep the heat, use the Spicy Pepper Syrup (page 166) instead of plain simple syrup.

55

Spritz Is a State of Mind

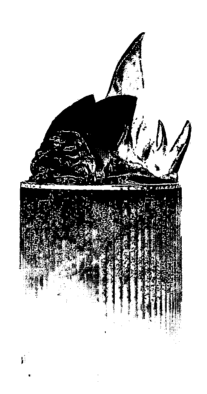

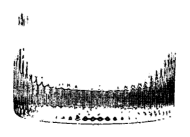

Maybe it's my Italian roots coming through, but I never get bored of a good spritz (they don't call me "the CEO of spritz season" for nothing). The bubbly Aperol Spritz (and others in the amaro category) falls into the category of the aperitivo, which comes from the Latin *aperire*, "to open," and helps stimulate one's appetite.

The recipes in this chapter stretch far beyond the usual Aperol territory, teaching you how to adjust to seasonal flavors and alternate liqueurs. As you'll come to discover, the spritz isn't about following one static recipe—it's a state of mind.

jules's
aperol spritz

Nothing transports me to Italy quite like a classic Aperol spritz. Thankfully, buying the ingredients for a spritz at home is a whole lot cheaper than buying a plane ticket. The bubbly, bitter, orange-scented drink is an aperitivo staple and just so happens to be the perfect way to refresh yourself at the end of a summer day. Like everything in life, there are good versions, and there are great versions. My take goes a little bit heavier on the Aperol than the prosecco to play up all those bitter, botanical notes. I also like to pour the prosecco into the glass first, followed by the Aperol and topped with the sparkling water for the most even distribution of bubbles. Whether you prefer this slightly bitter spritz or the traditional 3:2:1 ratio, be ready to make multiple, as the spritz effect is a real phenomenon!

Standard ice cubes, for serving

3 ounces prosecco

2½ ounces Aperol

1 ounce sparkling water, for topping

Fresh orange wheel, for garnish

Fill a wine glass with ice. In this order, add the prosecco, Aperol, and sparkling water. Give it a quick swizzle with a barspoon. Add an orange wheel and serve.

limoncello spritz

Limoncello gets a lot of credit as an after-dinner drink, and I have nothing against that. It's sweet, with a citrusy, bitter, palate-cleansing quality that hits the spot after a heavy meal. The liqueur is underrated, however, as a refreshing aperitif, which is why I feature it as the boozy backbone in this spritz. Fresh thyme lends an herbal, faintly savory scent. I love to make this spritz in the beginning of spring, once my late-winter batch of Homemade Citrus-cello (page 138) has finished steeping.

Standard ice cubes, for serving

3 ounces prosecco (try Riondo prosecco)

1½ ounces Homemade Citrus-cello (page 138) or store-bought limoncello

2 ounces club soda

Fresh lemon wheel, for garnish

Thyme sprig, for garnish

Fill a wine glass with ice. Add the prosecco, limoncello, and club soda and give it a gentle stir with a barspoon. Garnish with a lemon wheel and a sprig of fresh thyme.

fro-secco spritz

MAKES 2 SPRITZES

Spritz traditionalists might take issue with me for my icy, blended variation on the spritz, but to them I say, "Relax. Take a sip. Embrace carefree vacation vibes." Thankfully, for this frozen spritz, you don't need to own a big commercial slushie machine—you just need a decent blender. While blending ice into a drink can sometimes dilute it, I opt for blending in frozen mango chunks and orange segments, which are a breeze to prep ahead of time. It's important to note that you need a large blender when blending carbonated ingredients. Otherwise you will need to blend without all the carbonated ingredients, like prosecco and club soda, and stir them into the drink at the end.

6 ounces prosecco (try La Marca prosecco)

5 ounces Aperol or Aperitivo Cappelletti

5 frozen orange segments (see Tip)

1 cup frozen mango chunks

½ cup crushed ice

4 ounces club soda

Fresh orange wheels, for garnish

Mint leaves, for garnish

In a blender, combine the prosecco, Aperol, frozen orange segments, frozen mango chunks, and ice and blend slowly growing to a medium-high speed until smooth.

Divide between two stemless wine glasses (standard white wine glasses or rocks glasses also work) and stir in the club soda. Garnish each with a fresh orange wheel and fresh mint leaves and serve with a straw.

FREEZING ORANGE SEGMENTS
Peel the orange and separate the orange into segments. Arrange the orange segments flat on a tray or plate, not touching one another, and place in the freezer until frozen solid. Once frozen, store in a zip-seal bag in the freezer.

62

the
apple-rol spritz

While it's easy to associate the rhubarb-like bittersweetness of Aperol with springtime, this aperitif has some muskier, woody notes that go surprisingly well with autumnal flavors like apple cider and fresh sage. This spritz leans into those cozy, cold-weather qualities, taking a few tips from a classic Paper Plane, which typically combines bourbon, Aperol, lemon juice, and an amaro. A few added bubbles keep the drink lively, sippable, and afternoon-friendly to go with that predinner snack.

Standard ice cubes, for serving

2 ounces sparkling wine (try Domaine Rolet Cremant du Jura Brut)

¾ ounce bourbon (try Basil Hayden)

1½ ounces Aperol

1 ounce apple cider

½ ounce freshly squeezed lemon juice

1 ounce sparkling water, for topping

Fresh apple slices, for garnish

Sage sprig, for garnish

Fill a highball glass with ice. Add the sparkling wine, bourbon, Aperol, apple cider, and lemon juice. Top with sparkling water and mix gently with a barspoon to combine. Add fresh apple slices and sage sprig inside the glass.

winter sbagliato

The Italian word *sbagliato* means "mistaken," so the Negroni Sbagliato can be interpreted as a broken Negroni, since the prosecco is taking the place of the traditional Negroni option, gin. With its heavy dose of Campari, a Negroni Sbagliato can be a bit bitter for some. So, complementing the ruby-red Campari with a splash of cranberry syrup adds a juicy quality to the drink without it veering too sweet. The result is an extremely approachable spritz that easily doubles as a sparkly red accessory for your next holiday party. You can make the cranberry syrup from scratch, or just skim a tablespoon of liquid from your next batch of cranberry sauce and dilute with 1 tablespoon hot water for an impromptu syrup.

Standard ice cubes, for serving

1 ounce prosecco (try Mionetto prosecco)

1 ounce Campari or Cappelletti

1 ounce sweet vermouth (try Cocchi)

½ ounce Cranberry Syrup (page 166)

2 ounces club soda

Orange swath, for garnish (see Do the Twist or Swath, page 28)

Rosemary sprig, for garnish

Fill a large wine glass with ice. Add the prosecco, Campari, sweet vermouth, cranberry syrup, and club soda and give the drink a stir with a barspoon. Rim the glass with an orange swath, place it into the glass, and add a sprig of rosemary.

bianco
spritz

MAKES 1 SPRITZ

Somewhere between a dirty martini and a sbagliato, the bianco spritz is light, floral, and ever-so-slightly savory from a splash of olive brine and a juicy green olive garnish. Light-bodied and fruity, a good dry vermouth rounds out the strong astringent booziness of gin or vodka. Here, it adds a smooth finish to the prosecco, too. Vermouth is a fortified wine with a shelf life of about 6 weeks, so if you're using a little bit here and there for a martini, this is another way to use it before the flavor starts to dull in your refrigerator (yes, you should be refrigerating your opened bottles of vermouth!). Serve this for a daytime gathering as a much more interesting and slightly delicate alternative to light beer.

Standard ice cubes, for serving

3 ounces prosecco
(try Avissi prosecco)

2 ounces dry vermouth
(try Lo-Fi dry vermouth)

3 dashes of orange bitters
(try Fee Brothers)

Splash of olive brine (optional)

1 ounce club soda, for topping

2 or 3 pitted green olives, for garnish

Fresh lemon wedge, for garnish

Fill a wine glass with ice. Add the prosecco, dry vermouth, orange bitters, and olive brine (if using) and stir together. Top with the club soda. Garnish with green olives on a cocktail pick resting on the lip of the glass and add a fresh lemon wedge.

sunset spritz

Campari is often paired with the mellow floral warmth of orange (think of the twist of orange peel that often comes floating in a Negroni), but if you ask me, this bitter spirit is practically tailor-made to be paired with the sweet bitterness of a fresh grapefruit. This spritz leans on the bittersweet duet of Campari and grapefruit, softened with a few ounces of dry white wine, and brought to effervescent life with a heavy splash of club soda. The stunning gradient of colors is enough to bring some sunshine to even the grayest of winter afternoons.

Standard ice cubes, for serving

3 ounces dry white wine (try a pinot grigio)

2 ounces Campari

½ ounces freshly squeezed grapefruit juice

½ ounce Plain Simple Syrup (page 160)

2 ounces club soda, for topping

Fresh grapefruit wheel, for garnish

Fill a wine glass with ice. Add the white wine, Campari, grapefruit juice, and simple syrup and give a gentle swizzle with a barspoon to combine. Top with club soda and add a thinly sliced fresh grapefruit wheel, or depending on the size of the glass, opt for a thinly sliced grapefruit wheel cut in half.

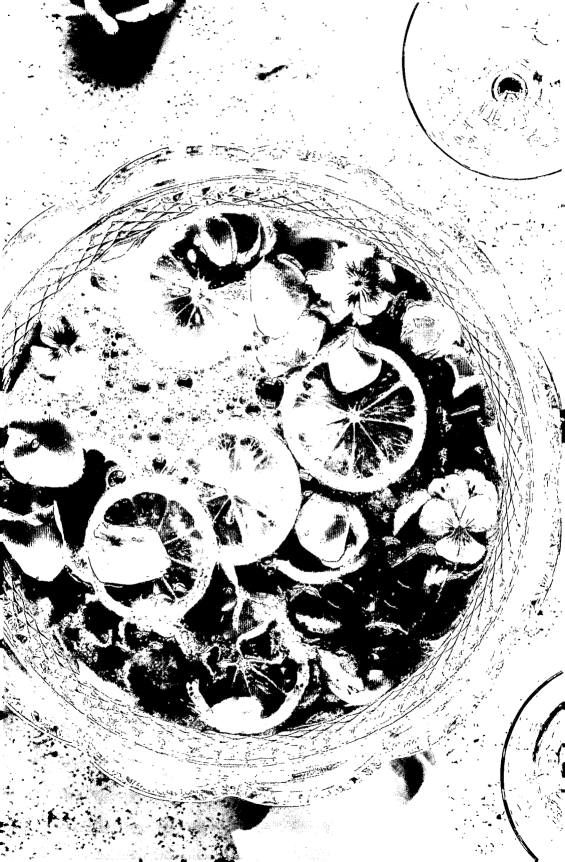

rosé all day spritz punch

This recipe reimagines the traditional spritz as a shareable party punch. Light, floral, fruity, and *very* pink, this is the perfect drink to serve at a Galentine's party, Mother's Day brunch, or a summer picnic. The rosé spritz is full of rosy colors from the fresh strawberries, sparkling rosé, and whichever edible flowers you choose for garnishing. Fresh strawberry puree packs a tart, bright punch—I like making this in the early summer, when the best strawberries start to hit the market.

1 cup hulled strawberries

½ cup cold filtered water

1 (750 ml) bottle sparkling rosé

1 cup Lillet Blanc (or Lillet Rosé if you want to lean into the pink)

1 cup freshly squeezed lemon juice (from about 5 large lemons)

½ cup Prosecco Syrup (page 164), or Plain Simple Syrup (page 160)

2 cups standard ice cubes, for the punch bowl

1 lemon, thinly sliced into wheels, for garnish (optional)

For each drink: standard ice cubes and 2 ounces club soda or prosecco

Edible flowers, such as food-grade rose petals or white violas, for garnish

In a blender, combine the strawberries and water and blend on medium-high speed until the mixture is smooth. Once blended, strain the mixture; you should have about 1½ cups.

Pour the 1½ cups strawberry puree into a large pitcher or punch bowl. Add the sparkling rosé, Lillet, lemon juice, and prosecco syrup. Stir and add the ice and lemon wheels (if using).

For each drink: Add some ice to a double rocks glass or stemless wine glass. Fill three-quarters of the way to the top with the punch (about 5 ounces per glass). Top with club soda or prosecco and serve garnished with an edible flower.

citrus party punch spritz

MAKES 12 SPRITZES

The spritz's easy-to-remember 3:2:1 ratio (3 parts prosecco, 2 parts Aperol, and 1 part club soda) makes it a no-brainer for scaling up as a party drink. This recipe takes inspiration from the classic spritz but adds a healthy dose of blood orange juice—if you can't find blood oranges, Cara Cara or navel oranges will be your best substitute. There's also an herbaceous touch from the gin and the thyme-infused simple syrup. This batched spritz won't just save you time making individual drinks, it also has the built-in convenience of using up a whole bottle of prosecco, meaning you won't be stuck with any half bottles of flat, lukewarm bubbly at the end of the party—just happy (and refreshed) guests.

2 cups Aperol

1 cup gin (try Malfy Gin con Arancia)

1 cup freshly squeezed blood orange juice (from about 3 large oranges)

½ cup thyme simple syrup (see Herbaceous Syrups, page 162)

1 cup club soda

1 (750 ml) bottle prosecco (try Scarpetta prosecco)

2 cups standard ice cubes, for the punch bowl, plus more for individual glasses

2 blood oranges, thinly sliced into wheels, for garnish

Edible flowers, such as pansies, for garnish (optional)

Thyme sprigs, for garnish

In a large punch bowl, combine the Aperol, gin, blood orange juice, and thyme syrup.

When ready to serve, add the club soda, prosecco, and ice and gently stir with a barspoon. Place a few orange wheels and edible flowers (if using) into the punch bowl.

For each drink: Fill a double rocks glass or stemless wine glass with ice. Ladle the punch over the ice to fill the glass and add fresh thyme sprigs and fresh blood orange wheels on top.

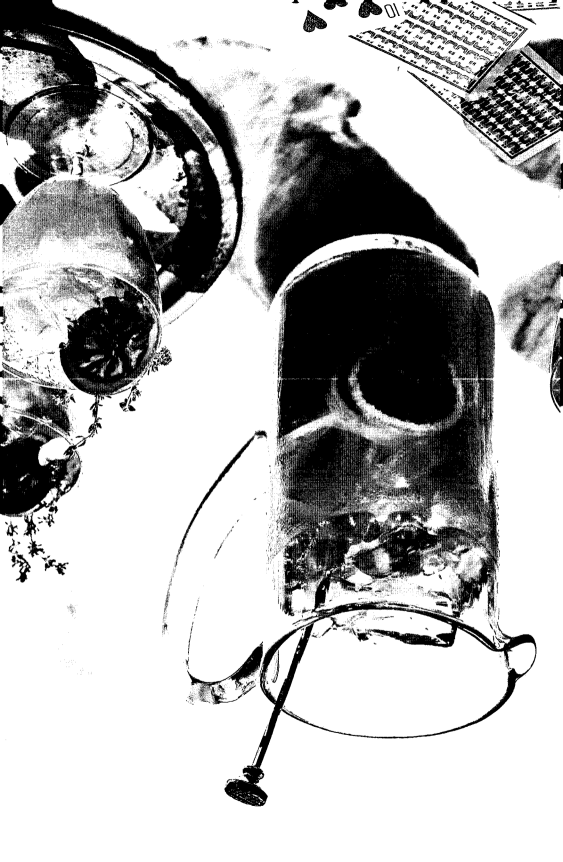

A Margarita
for Every Mood

Nothing against martinis and manhattans, but if there's one classic cocktail I think everyone should know how to prepare at home, it's the margarita. Once you make yourself a good one for the first time, those neon-green bottles of dive-bar margarita mix will become a distant memory, and you will have the power to summon salty, citrusy vacation vibes at the drop of a hat.

This chapter is designed to turn you into a margarita pro. First, I'll teach you how to make the Platonic ideal of the drink, and then how to remake and reshape the drink for any possible mood you could be in. I strongly believe in making drinks how you like them, so feel free to swap tequila for your favorite smoky mezcal or play with the sweetness levels by adding a little extra syrup. You'll notice the use of agave syrup rather than simple syrup; that's because it complements those natural agave flavors of tequila and mezcal, intensifying the overall taste with a deeper and slightly sweeter flavor.

classic margarita

MAKES 1 MARGARITA

Margaritas live in the category of sour cocktails—drinks that bring together a spirit, a citrus, and a sweetener in a delicate balancing act that manages to stimulate all your taste buds with every sip. In a margarita, this means tequila, lime juice, and orange liqueur. With just three ingredients (plus a touch of salt to rim the glass), this is a drink worth memorizing. Pick an additive-free tequila blanco that you like enough to drink on its own, and whatever you do, make sure you're using freshly squeezed lime juice. Everyone has their personal preferences when it comes to the salted rim, but personally, I like to coat half of the rim with salt so that I can customize every single sip to be just as salty as I feel like.

For the rim: lime wedge and kosher salt

2 ounces tequila blanco (try El Tesoro)

1 ounce orange liqueur (try Cointreau)

¾ ounce freshly squeezed lime juice

Standard ice cubes, for shaking

Cracked ice, for serving

Fresh lime wheel, for garnish

Run the lime wedge around the outer rim of a rocks glass. Roll the outer rim of the glass in the salt (try not to get any salt on the inner rim of the glass, see A Rimmed Glass, page 28). Place the rimmed glass in the freezer to chill.

In a cocktail shaker, combine the tequila, orange liqueur, and lime juice. Add ice, cover, and shake vigorously for 30 seconds.

Add freshly cracked ice to the chilled salt-rimmed glass. Double-strain the margarita into the glass. Serve with a fresh lime wheel on top.

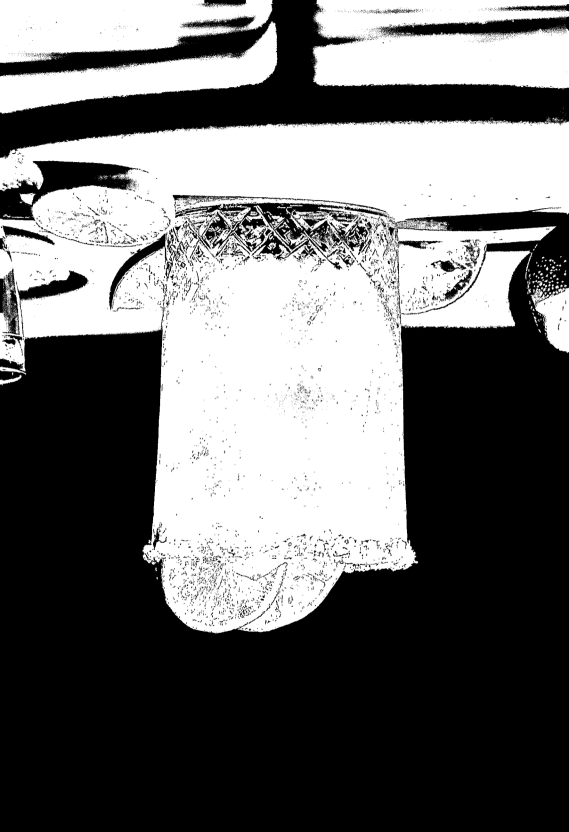

coconut aperol margarita

While Aperol might not be the first spirit you think to add to a margarita, its bittersweet orange zest notes play harmoniously with the orange liqueur and lime juice. As the crowned "CEO of spritz season" and "margarita queen," I think this dreamy coral anomaly of a cocktail checks all the right boxes.

For the rim: lime wedge and chile salt

1½ ounces tequila blanco (try G4)

1 ounce Strawberry-Infused Aperol (recipe follows) or regular Aperol

¾ ounce orange liqueur (try Cointreau)

¾ ounce canned coconut milk (try Thai Kitchen)

¾ ounce freshly squeezed lime juice

½ ounce Plain Simple Syrup (page 160)

Standard ice cubes, for shaking and serving

Fresh lime wheel, for garnish

Edible flowers, such as marigolds, for garnish (optional)

Strawberry-Infused Aperol

12 ounces Aperol (about half a bottle)

10 medium strawberries, hulled and halved

Run the lime wedge around the outer rim of a rocks glass. Roll the outer rim of the glass in the chile salt (try not to get any salt on the inner rim of the glass, see A Rimmed Glass, page 28). Place the rimmed glass in the freezer to chill.

In a cocktail shaker, combine the tequila, Aperol, orange liqueur, coconut milk, lime juice, and simple syrup. Add ice, cover, and shake vigorously for 30 seconds. Add ice to the chilled glass and strain the margarita over the ice. Add a fresh lime wheel on the rim of the glass and, if desired, a marigold for garnish.

Strawberry-Infused Aperol

MAKES ABOUT 1½ CUPS (12 OUNCES)

Pour the Aperol into a clean jar with a tight-fitting lid, add the strawberries, and set aside in a cool, dark place for 8 hours or overnight.

Strain the mixture through a fine-mesh sieve set over a medium bowl; discard the strawberries (or reserve for a boozy strawberry puree). Funnel the infused Aperol back into the container and store in a cool, dark place for up to 6 months. (Try using this strawberry-infused Aperol for your next Aperol Spritz, page 58.)

pineapple mezcal margarita

If you've ever squeezed a lime wedge over some sliced pineapple and doused the whole thing in salty, spicy Tajín, then you know that a touch of heat can bring tropical fruit alive. Here, tart fresh pineapple juice teams up with mezcal and habanero syrup for a drink that's warm in spirit but cooling enough for any hot day. Since you'll be cutting into a pineapple to make fresh pineapple juice, this is a great opportunity to flex your garnish skills with a dehydrated pineapple flower.

For the rim: lime wedge and chile salt

2 ounces mezcal (try Mezcal 400 Conejos Espadin)

1½ ounces Fresh Pineapple Juice (recipe follows)

¾ ounce orange liqueur (try dry Curaçao)

¾ ounce freshly squeezed lime juice

½ ounce habanero syrup (see Spicy Pepper Syrup, page 166)

Standard ice cubes, for shaking

1 large square ice cube, for serving

Dehydrated pineapple flowers (see Dehydrate Those Slices, page 29), for garnish

Fresh Pineapple Juice

½ fresh pineapple, peeled, cored, and cut into bite-size chunks

½ cup cold filtered water

Run the lime wedge around the outer rim of a rocks glass. Roll the outer rim of the glass in the salt (try not to get any salt on the inner rim of the glass, see A Rimmed Glass, page 28). Place the rimmed glass in the freezer to chill.

In a cocktail shaker, combine the mezcal, pineapple juice, orange liqueur, lime juice, and habanero syrup. Add ice, cover, and shake vigorously for 30 seconds. Double-strain the cocktail into your chilled glass over the large ice cube. Add a dehydrated pineapple flower inside the glass.

Fresh Pineapple Juice

MAKES ABOUT 2½ CUPS (20 OUNCES)

In a blender, combine the pineapple chunks and water and blend until completely smooth with no chunks of fruit. Strain through a fine-mesh sieve set over a liquid measuring cup. Transfer to a clean airtight container and store in the fridge up to 1 week.

82

avocado margarita

If you've ever had an avocado blended into a smoothie, you know that this green addition is way more about the texture than the taste. Here it adds a silky, creaminess to a spicy blended marg while managing to taste surprisingly light. The whole drink has a refreshingly savory bent from a sprig of fresh cilantro, a dash of jalapeño simple syrup, and a salty rim. Preferably serve with some salty tortilla chips on the side.

For the rim: lime wedge and lime zest salt

½ avocado, pitted

2 ounces tequila reposado (try Volcan)

¾ ounce freshly squeezed lime juice

¾ ounce orange liqueur (try Cointreau)

½ ounce jalapeño syrup (see Spicy Pepper Syrup, page 166)

1 cilantro sprig (including the stem)

1 cup standard ice cubes, for blending

Small cilantro sprig, for garnish

Fresh lime wheel, for garnish

Run the lime wedge around the outer rim of a rocks glass or margarita. Roll the outer rim of the glass in the lime zest salt (try not to get any salt on the inner rim of the glass, see A Rimmed Glass, page 28). Place the rimmed glass in the freezer to chill.

Scoop the avocado into a blender. Add the tequila, lime juice, orange liqueur, pepper syrup, cilantro, and the ice and blend until the mixture has reached a smooth, milkshake-like consistency, about 1 minute.

Pour the margarita into the prepared glass. Garnish with a cilantro sprig and lime wheel.

WANT TO LEVEL UP YOUR NEXT AVOCADO MARGARITA?
Try making an avocado-infused tequila by blending 1 avocado with 8 ounces blanco tequila (it's best used within 2 days of making). Use this avocado-infused tequila as directed in this recipe, but omit the avocado, and shake the ingredients rather than blending them.

carrot margarita

If you're in the habit of getting your weekly carrot intake in the form of roasted veggies and crudités, it's time to introduce this earthy root vegetable into your cocktail routine. Carrots produce a juice that's lightly sweet, extremely refreshing, and vividly orange, and the best part is you don't even need a juicer to make it—just a blender and a sieve. In this margarita, the carrot juice adds a springy freshness to the mix of tequila, lime juice, agave, and orange liqueur.

For the rim: lime wedge, chile salt, and kosher salt

2 ounces Fresh Carrot Juice (recipe follows)

1½ ounces tequila blanco (try El Tequileño)

¾ ounce freshly squeezed lime juice

¾ ounce orange liqueur (try Cointreau)

½ ounce agave syrup

Standard ice cubes, for shaking and serving

Edible flowers, such as marigolds, or carrot tops, for garnish

Fresh lime wheel, for garnish

Fresh Carrot Juice

2 cups chopped carrots (about 4 medium carrots)

½ cup cold filtered water

Run the lime wedge around the outer rim of a rocks glass. Roll the outer rim of the glass in a mixture of chile salt and kosher salt (try not to get any salt on the inner rim of the glass, see A Rimmed Glass, page 28). Place the rimmed glass in the freezer to chill.

In a cocktail shaker, combine the carrot juice, tequila, lime juice, orange liqueur, and agave. Add ice, cover, and shake vigorously for 30 seconds. Strain into the prepared glass over ice and add edible flowers or baby carrots on top of the glass and a lime wheel on the rim of the glass.

Fresh Carrot Juice

MAKES ABOUT 1½ CUPS (12 OUNCES)

In a blender, combine the carrots and water and blend until smooth. Strain through a fine-mesh sieve into a jar or other lidded container. Keep refrigerated until ready to use; it will last about 1 week.

blended
tropical margarita

This frozen marg is so luxuriously thick and creamy that you could almost eat it with a spoon. While it's easy for blended drinks to get watery and diluted after a few minutes in the sun, this one bypasses that possibility by using frozen cubes of mango and pineapple instead of the usual handfuls of ice cubes for blending. If you're not already keeping your freezer stocked with frozen chopped fruit, today's the day to begin. Freezing your favorite fruit will seriously transform both your morning smoothie routine as well as your evening cocktail game.

For the rim: lime wedge and
    chile salt

4 ounces tequila blanco
    (try Mijenta)

1½ ounces orange liqueur
    (try dry Curaçao)

2 ounces Fresh Pineapple Juice
    (page 82) or ½ cup frozen
    pineapple chunks

1½ ounces freshly squeezed
    lime juice

1 cup frozen mango chunks

1 ounce agave syrup

½ cup crushed ice cubes

Pinch of kosher salt

Optional garnishes: fresh lime
    wheels, mango slices, and/or
    pineapple leaves

Run the lime wedge around the outer rims of two rocks glasses. Roll the outer rims of the glasses in the chile salt (try not to get any salt on the inner rim of the glass, see A Rimmed Glass, page 28). Place the rimmed glasses in the freezer to chill.

In a blender, combine the tequila, orange liqueur, pineapple juice, lime juice, mango, agave syrup, ice, and salt and blend until smooth, 1 to 2 minutes. Pour into the prepared glasses and garnish with fresh lime wheels, mango slices, and/or pineapple leaves on top, if desired.

the paloma-rita sour

The margarita is a not-so-distant cousin of the whiskey sour, as both are part of the "sour" category (see page 12). For most sour cocktails, you can add an egg white to bring some velvety body, and the margarita is no exception. This one celebrates the grapefruit flavor you'd taste in a typical Paloma but adds a fluffy mouthfeel that rounds out the acidity of the drink, thanks to the egg white. To do a "dry shake," which is often called for in recipes with egg whites so they properly froth, just shake your ingredients vigorously for 20 seconds before adding ice. After a dry shake, add one large cube and a generous handful of standard ice cubes, cover, and shake hard enough so that you can hear the ice cubes clanging from one end of the shaker to the other, about 30 seconds.

For the rim: lime wedge and chile salt or kosher salt

1½ ounces tequila blanco (try Lalo)

½ ounce mezcal (optional; try Del Maguey Vida Clásico)

1 ounce freshly squeezed grapefruit juice   ·

¾ ounce freshly squeezed lime juice

¾ ounce orange liqueur (try Cointreau)

½ ounce agave syrup

1 large egg white or 2 tablespoons aquafaba

1 large ice cube plus a handful of standard ice cubes, for shaking

Fresh grapefruit wedge, for garnish

Run the lime wedge around the outer rim of a coupe or Nick & Nora glass. Roll the outer rim of the glass in the chile salt (try not to get any salt on the inner rim of the glass, see A Rimmed Glass, page 28). Place the rimmed glass in the freezer to chill.

In a cocktail shaker, combine the tequila, mezcal (if using), grapefruit juice, lime juice, orange liqueur, agave, and egg white (make sure that there are no bits of yolk; the fat will prevent the white from getting frothy). Cover and dry shake (without ice) vigorously for 20 seconds to froth the egg white (or use a hand frother if you have one).

Add the large ice cube and standard ice cubes, cover, and shake again vigorously for 30 seconds. Double-strain into the rimmed glass. Garnish with a fresh grapefruit wedge.

blood orange thyme margarita

Bartenders love reaching for a blood orange for its vivid red color, but the citrus also has a flavor that's unmatched by any other variety of orange—it's tart, ever-so-slightly bitter, and full of mellow, stone fruit–like sweetness. When blood oranges are in season, I love stocking up, juicing them, and freezing some of the juice for the months ahead. Here the fruit's unique tartness works its way into a spicy, smoky margarita that leans a little bit savory thanks to the chile liqueur and thyme simple syrup.

For the rim: lime wedge and fresh thyme leaves mixed with kosher salt

1½ ounces mezcal (try Agua Magica)

¾ ounce freshly squeezed blood orange juice

¾ ounce freshly squeezed lime juice

½ ounce chile liqueur

½ ounce thyme simple syrup (see Herbaceous Syrups, page 162)

Pinch of kosher salt

Standard ice cubes, for shaking

Freshly cracked ice or standard ice cubes, for serving

2 ounces sparkling water, for topping

Dehydrated orange slice (see Dehydrate Those Slices, page 29), for garnish

Edible flowers, such as violas, for garnish (optional)

Run the lime wedge around the outer rim of a rocks glass. Roll the outer rim of the glass in the thyme leaves mixed with kosher salt (try not to get any on the inner rim of the glass, see A Rimmed Glass, page 28). Place the rimmed glass in the freezer to chill.

In a cocktail shaker, combine the mezcal, blood orange juice, lime juice, chile liqueur, thyme syrup, and kosher salt. Add ice, cover, and shake vigorously for 30 seconds. Fill the chilled glass with freshly cracked or standard ice cubes. Double-strain the cocktail over the ice. Top with sparkling water. Garnish with a dehydrated citrus wheel on top and/or fresh violas.

pantry margarita

This margarita makes the most of what's already sitting in your pantry (or refrigerator), no customized simple syrup required. Just reach for your favorite jar of jam, shake a tablespoon in with the rest of the ingredients, and strain into a glass. A vigorous shake will distribute that fruity flavor (and color) throughout your drink, and a double-strain will make sure that none of the little solid pieces of fruit make it into your finished cocktail. Try this with any jam, jelly, marmalade, or preserves. If you have a jar that's almost empty, you can even build your cocktail in the jar, twist on the lid, and shake it right in there.

For the rim: lime wedge and lime zest kosher salt

1½ ounces tequila blanco (try Tapatío)

¾ ounce orange liqueur (try Cointreau)

¾ ounce freshly squeezed lime juice

1 tablespoon blackberry jam or preserves of your choice

Standard ice cubes, for shaking

1 large ice cube, for serving

Fresh or dehydrated lime wheel (see Dehydrate Those Slices, page 29), for garnish

2 fresh blackberries (or other seasonal ingredient; see Tip), for garnish

Run the lime wedge around the outer rim of a rocks glass. Roll the outer rim of the glass in the lime zest kosher salt (try not to get any salt on the inner rim of the glass, see A Rimmed Glass, page 28). Place the rimmed glass in the freezer to chill.

In a cocktail shaker, combine the tequila, orange liqueur, lime juice, and blackberry jam. Add ice, cover, and shake vigorously for 30 seconds to ensure the jam is fully incorporated. Double-strain into the rimmed rocks glass over large ice cube. Garnish with a lime wheel and 2 blackberries on a cocktail pick.

GARNISH FOR EVERY SEASON
When adding a flavored simple syrup—even one made with jam!—to a cocktail, consider garnishing with the fresh version of the fruit used. For example, if you're using strawberry preserves, garnish with a fresh strawberry, or try sliced jalapeños if you're using pepper jelly.

94

tangy tamarind punch

With its puckeringly sour flavor and earthy brown–sugar sweetness, tamarind can add a lot of complexity to a drink. You can use store-bought tamarind concentrate or make your own starting with tamarind pods (see below).

For the rims: lime wedges and chile salt

1½ cups tequila blanco (try Don Fulano)

1 cup tamarind concentrate

½ cup freshly squeezed lime juice (from about 6 large limes)

½ cup orange liqueur (try Cointreau)

½ cup agave syrup, plus more as needed (optional)

5 cups standard ice cubes, for blending

Dehydrated lime wheels (see Dehydrate Those Slices, page 29), for garnish

Homemade Tamarind Concentrate

12 tamarind pods

3 cups filtered water

Run lime wedges around the outer rims of eight rocks glasses. Roll the outer rims of the glasses in the salt (see A Rimmed Glass, page 28).

In a large blender, combine the tequila, tamarind concentrate, lime juice, orange liqueur, agave syrup (if using), and ice and blend until smooth. Pour into the prepared glasses and top each glass with a dehydrated lime wheel.

Homemade Tamarind Concentrate

MAKES 3 CUPS

Remove the brittle outer shells of the tamarind pods. Pull out the fibrous fruit wrapped around the seeds.

In a medium saucepan, bring the water to a boil. Add the tamarind, reduce to a simmer, and cook until it's soft, about 10 minutes.

Remove from the heat and cool to room temperature. Once the liquid is cool, pick out the seeds with your hands and discard.

Add the liquid and fruit to a blender and blend until smooth. Refrigerate in a tightly sealed container for up to 3 weeks.

Start the Party
on a High Note

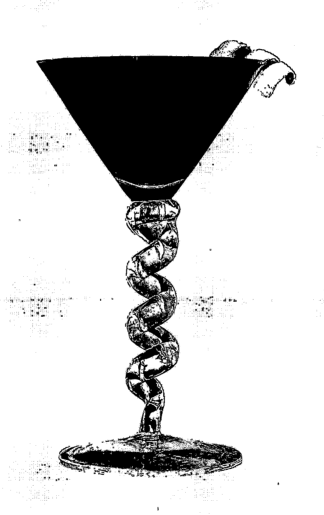

There's an oft-repeated adage about entertaining: As long as you hand every guest a drink the moment they walk in the door, the party is set to go off without a hitch. I suggest taking this a step further and say that if you can hand every guest a well-balanced, freshly made, pristinely garnished *cocktail* upon arrival, it will be an extra-good party!

This chapter is a celebration of those first few memorable sips of the evening—the drinks that get the conversation flowing, possibly even while buying you some extra time to put the finishing touches on that cheese board or those crudités. You can weave in some seasonal freshness with a round of Persimmon Mezcal Sours (page 115) or flex your glass-smoking skills with the Smoked Rosemary Negroni Sour (page 108). If a big, low-maintenance, make-ahead batch is more your speed, try The Weekenders' Party Punch (page 119) or Winter Spice Sangria (page 120).

olive oil martini

If you always order your martini dirty with extra olives, this martini is for you. To incorporate some grassy olive oil notes, I use a technique called fat-washing. All this entails is infusing the spirit with some of your best olive oil. You'll be left with a beautifully savory cocktail that's tailor-made for your next steak night or spaghetti date night.

3 ounces Olive Oil–Infused Gin (or vodka; recipe follows)

¾ ounce dry vermouth (try Lo-Fi)

2 dashes of orange bitters

Pinch of sea salt

Standard ice cubes, for mixing

3 green olives, such as Castelvetrano, on a cocktail pick, for garnish

2 or 3 drops of olive oil, for garnish (optional)

Olive Oil–Infused Gin (or Vodka)

2 ounces extra-virgin olive oil (use the good stuff here)

1½ cups London dry gin (try Sipsmith) or vodka (try Kástra Elión)

Rosemary sprig (optional)

Place a mixing glass and a coupe or martini glass in the freezer to chill.

Once chilled, add the olive oil–infused gin, the vermouth, bitters, and salt.

Add ice cubes and stir swiftly with a barspoon for about 20 seconds to chill and slightly dilute.

Strain into the chilled glass and place the olives on a cocktail pick on the rim of the glass. If desired, add a few drops of olive oil on top.

Olive Oil–Infused Gin (or Vodka)

MAKES 1½ CUPS (12 OUNCES)

In a jar with a tight-fitting lid, combine the extra-virgin olive oil, gin, and rosemary and gently shake together. Cover and set aside for at least 12 hours in a cool, dark place.

After 12 hours, place the jar in the freezer until the olive oil has solidified, about 2 hours. Strain through a fine-mesh sieve lined with cheesecloth, discarding the solidified olive oil and rosemary.

Store in an airtight container or funnel into an empty gin bottle and place in the freezer until ready to use.

100

apricot french 75

A traditional French 75 brings together a celebratory mix of Champagne, gin, lemon juice, and simple syrup. My early summer spin on the fizzy classic gets its sunset hue from a lightning-fast apricot puree and a boost of herbal sweetness from a basil simple syrup (page 162). Opt for a botanical-leaning gin to complement the floral qualities of the apricot and basil, and a dry Champagne to counter the sweetness of the apricot. If you can't find apricots, try this with plums.

2 ounces gin (try Barr Hill)

¾ ounce freshly squeezed lemon juice

½ ounce Apricot Puree (recipe follows)

½ ounce basil simple syrup (see Herbaceous Syrups, page 162)

½ ounce amaretto

Standard ice cubes, for shaking

2 ounces dry Champagne (or enough to fill glass)

Edible flowers, such as violas, or a fresh lemon twist (see Do the Twist or Swath, page 28), for garnish

Apricot Puree

5 ripe medium apricots, halved and pitted

½ cup filtered water

Place a coupe glass in the freezer to chill.

In a cocktail shaker, combine the gin, lemon juice, apricot puree, basil syrup, and amaretto. Add ice, cover, and shake vigorously for about 30 seconds. Double-strain into the chilled coupe glass. Top with Champagne and garnish with 1 or 2 viola blossoms or a lemon twist.

Apricot Puree

MAKES ABOUT 1 CUP (8 OUNCES)

In a blender, combine the apricots and water and puree until smooth. Refrigerate in a sealed container until ready to use. Hang on to any leftovers for cocktails and smoothies; it will hold for up to 2 weeks.

passion fruit martini

MAKES 1 COCKTAIL

Here is my refreshing take on The Pornstar Martini. You might notice that this drink has a frothy, foamy texture, and believe it or not, this is just from the aeration of shaking the pineapple juice with ice—a trick borrowed from classic cocktails like the Garibaldi (4 ounces fresh orange juice and 1½ ounces Campari). If you want to be extra with the presentation here, garnish with half of a passion fruit and serve with a sidecar shot of prosecco!

2 ounces vanilla vodka, store-bought or homemade (see below)

1 ounce Fresh Pineapple Juice (page 82)

¾ ounce passion fruit liqueur

½ ounce freshly squeezed lime juice

½ ounce Vanilla Syrup (page 163)

1 passion fruit

Standard ice cubes, for shaking

Edible flowers, for garnish

½ passion fruit, for garnish (optional)

1 shot of prosecco (optional)

Place a coupe glass in the freezer to chill.

In a cocktail shaker, combine the vanilla vodka, pineapple juice, passion fruit liqueur, lime juice, and vanilla syrup. Cut the passion fruit in half and scoop the insides into the cocktail shaker. Add ice, cover, and shake vigorously for 30 seconds. Double-strain into the chilled coupe glass. Gently place the edible flowers and passion fruit half (if using) on top. Serve with a shot of prosecco, if desired.

Vanilla Vodka

MAKES 750 ML VANILLA VODKA

Add two halved vanilla beans to a 750 ml bottle of vodka, replace to top, and infuse for 10 to 14 days, gently shaking every other day. Don't let the vanilla infuse for too long, as the vodka can take on an undesirable vanilla extract-like flavor.

Strain through a fine-mesh sieve into a 4-cup liquid measuring cup. Funnel it back into the vodka bottle, cover, and store in a cool dark place. This will last indefinitely.

104

kentucky jungle bird

MAKES 1 COCKTAIL

The jungle bird is a rare situation in the world of classic cocktails, where you'll see bracingly bitter Campari paired with tropical pineapple juice for a perfect harmony of bitter, sweet, and tangy. My version swaps out the usual rum for the slightly drier alternative of bourbon. Like rum, bourbon has complexity and layers, and the spirit's roundness makes it a great match for pineapple juice. Make a batch of these for a backyard barbecue or a midwinter gathering when you're craving a taste of tropical sunshine. To really take things up a notch, try the flaming sugar cube garnish.

1½ ounces bourbon (try Yellowstone Select)

¾ ounce Campari

1½ ounces Fresh Pineapple Juice (page 82)

¾ ounce freshly squeezed lime juice

½ ounce Plain Simple Syrup (page 160)

½ ounce passion fruit liqueur

Standard ice cubes, for shaking

Cracked ice or 1 large ice cube, for serving

Pineapple leaves, for garnish

Fresh lime wheel or flaming sugar cube (see Get Fired Up, page 29), for garnish

In a cocktail shaker, combine the bourbon, Campari, pineapple juice, lime juice, simple syrup, and passion fruit liqueur. Add ice, cover, and shake vigorously for 30 seconds. Double-strain into a double rocks glass with freshly cracked ice or a large cube.

Add 2 pineapple leaves to the glass. Add a flaming sugar cube.

smoked rosemary negroni sour

In a booze-forward drink like the Negroni, the untraditional ingredients in this recipe, like the lemon juice, add freshness, and egg white rounds out the bitter edges of the spirits. Woven through each sip is just a subtle hint of rosemary and a whisper of smoke. It's so easy to incorporate smoke into a cocktail—you don't need any special equipment either. Just a lighter and a rosemary sprig season the glass with a piney-smoky scent that transforms each sip.

Rosemary sprigs

1 large egg white or
  2 tablespoons aquafaba

½ ounce freshly squeezed
  lemon juice

½ ounce freshly squeezed
  orange juice

½ ounce rosemary simple syrup
  (see Herbaceous Syrups,
  page 162)

1 ounce Campari

1 ounce sweet vermouth (try
  Carpano Antica)

1 ounce gin (try Hendrick's Gin)

Standard ice cubes, for shaking

Fresh or dehydrated orange wheel
  (see Dehydrate Those Slices,
  page 29), for garnish

Select a martini or coupe glass and cut a fresh rosemary sprig to fit inside the glass to ensure the rosemary is enclosed. In a well-ventilated area, use a kitchen torch or lighter to light the tip of the rosemary until it starts to smoke. Place on a heatproof surface (like a sheet pan) and overturn the glass on top so that the rosemary is enclosed. Let the glass fill with smoke for 2 minutes and then place it in the freezer to chill.

In a cocktail shaker, combine the egg white (make sure that there are no bits of yolk; the fat will prevent the white from getting frothy), lemon juice, orange juice, rosemary syrup, Campari, vermouth, and gin. Cover and dry shake (without ice) vigorously for 20 seconds to froth the egg white (or use a hand frother if you have one). Add some ice, cover, and shake again vigorously for 30 seconds. Double-strain into the smoked and chilled glass.

Gently place an orange wheel to float in the middle of the froth and/or a rosemary sprig on top.

lychee martini

This pearlescent little number is one of the most highly requested drinks among my friends. I prefer vodka to gin to let the lychee juice shine, and the lemon juice cuts through the candy-like sweetness of the lychee. Whenever I see canned lychees, I always stock up for my next batch, but you can easily find canned lychees online. A pinch of edible glitter, which can also be purchased online, can add some heavy-duty glamor!

2 ounces vodka (try Haku vodka)

1 ounce lychee juice (from a can of lychees)

¾ ounce freshly squeezed lemon juice

½ ounce elderflower liqueur (try St-Germain)

1 barspoon edible glitter (optional)

Standard ice cubes, for shaking

Lychee fruit, for garnish

Edible flowers, such as violas, for garnish (optional)

Place a martini glass or coupe in the freezer to chill.

In a cocktail shaker, combine the vodka, lychee juice, lemon juice, elderflower liqueur, and edible glitter (if using). Add ice, cover, and shake vigorously for 30 seconds. Double-strain into the chilled martini or coupe glass. Using a cocktail pick, skewer 2 or 3 lychee fruit and rest them on the side of the rim and/or add fresh violas on top.

stone fruit whiskey sour

Once you get the hang of a classic whiskey sour, it's fun to dream up seasonal variations. This riff is designed to help you dance your way through a whole summer's worth of stone fruit. The caramelly bourbon and herbaceous basil are the perfect sunny accompaniments to stone fruit. Feel inspired to let your local farmers' market be your guide.

2 ounces bourbon (try Angel's Envy)

1 ounce Stone Fruit Puree (recipe follows)

¾ ounce freshly squeezed lemon juice

½ ounce basil simple syrup (see Herbaceous Syrups, page 162)

3 fresh basil leaves

1 large egg white or 2 tablespoons aquafaba

Standard ice cubes, for shaking

Seasonal Whiskey Sour Variations

Fall Fig: Swap figs for the stone fruit and puree. Substitute maple syrup for the basil syrup and leaves.

Winter Pomegranate: Swap the stone fruit puree for pomegranate juice, the basil leaves for fresh rosemary leaves, and the basil syrup for rosemary syrup. Garnish with a rosemary sprig.

Spring Strawberry Basil: Swap the stone fruit puree for a strawberry puree.

Place a coupe or rocks glass in the freezer to chill.

In a cocktail shaker, combine the bourbon, stone fruit puree, lemon juice, basil syrup, 2 of the basil leaves, and the egg white (make sure that there are no bits of yolk; the fat will prevent the white from getting frothy). Cover and dry shake (without ice) vigorously for 20 seconds to froth the egg white (or use a hand frother if you have one). Add ice, cover, and shake vigorously again for 30 seconds.

Double-strain into the chilled glass and garnish with the remaining basil leaf.

Stone Fruit Puree

MAKES ABOUT 1 CUP (8 OUNCES)

In a blender, combine 1 cup of chopped nectarines (or any stone fruit) and ½ cup cold water and blend until the mixture has a smooth consistency. Refrigerate in an airtight container up to 2 weeks.

persimmon mezcal sour

MAKES 1 COCKTAIL

This drink is a perfect celebration of the sweet, honey-melon flavors of persimmon—a fruit with a fleeting, late-fall harvest season. When shopping, look for fruit that's slightly firm with a tiny bit of give, almost the way you might shop for a perfectly ripe avocado. When persimmons aren't in season, feel free to try this one with plums, apricot, or even mango.

1 ounce Persimmon Puree (recipe follows)

1 large egg white or 2 tablespoons aquafaba

½ ounce Persimmon Syrup (page 165)

¾ ounce freshly squeezed lime juice

½ ounce freshly squeezed grapefruit juice

2 ounces mezcal (try La Luna)

Standard ice cubes, for shaking

Thin slice of persimmon, for garnish

Persimmon Puree

2 Fuyu (nonastringent) persimmons, quartered

½ cup cold filtered water

Place a coupe glass in the freezer to chill.

In a cocktail shaker, combine the persimmon puree, egg white (make sure that there are no bits of yolk; the fat will prevent the white from getting frothy), persimmon syrup, lime juice, grapefruit juice, and mezcal. Cover and dry shake (without ice) vigorously for 20 seconds to froth the egg white (or use a hand frother if you have one).

Add the ice to the shaker, cover, and shake vigorously again for 30 seconds. Double-strain into the chilled coupe glass and gently place a persimmon slice on top of the foam.

Persimmon Puree

I like using this puree for seasonal margaritas or morning smoothies.

MAKES ABOUT 1 CUP (8 OUNCES)

Stem the persimmons and rinse the fruit. In a blender, combine the persimmons and water and blend until smooth. Refrigerate in an airtight container until ready to use. It will keep for up to 2 weeks.

the vacationer's last word

A classic Last Word brings together gin, lime juice, green Chartreuse, and Maraschino liqueur—but here I depart from the traditional gin and instead add the gently sweet vacation vibe of white rum. It's one of my favorite drinks to make for guests because as an equal parts–style cocktail, it's impossible to mess up. The smooth fruitiness of Maraschino liqueur tempers some of the bitter notes in the rum and Chartreuse, and a splash of Cava elongates each sip.

¾ ounce white rum (try Don Q Cristal)

¾ ounce freshly squeezed lime juice

¾ ounce green Chartreuse

¾ ounce Maraschino liqueur (try Luxardo)

Standard ice cubes, for shaking

2 ounces Cava (try Juvé & Camps), for topping

Fresh lime twist (see Do the Twist or Swath, page 28), for garnish

Place a coupe glass in the freezer to chill.

In a cocktail shaker, combine the rum, lime juice, Chartreuse, and Maraschino liqueur. Add ice, cover, and shake vigorously for 30 seconds. Double-strain into the chilled coupe glass. Top with Cava and place a fresh lime twist on the rim of the glass.

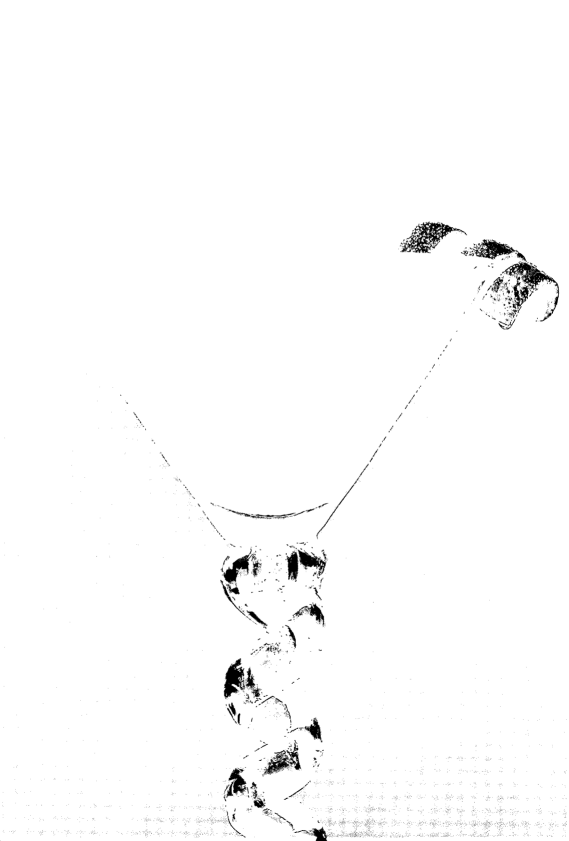

the weekenders' party punch

MAKES 12 COCKTAILS

Think of this punch as the bubbly, bright friend you can invite to any party. Best of all, you can swap in the spirit of your choice for the tequila blanco or vodka—or you could just create a station around the punch bowl to customize their own glass. This drink is a great excuse to dust off your prettiest Bundt cake mold for a big flower-studded ice ring.

Ice Ring

1 orange, 1 lemon, and 1 lime, thinly sliced

8 to 10 fresh mint leaves

8 to 10 edible flowers

Punch

2 cups freshly squeezed grapefruit juice or blood orange juice (from about 4 grapefruits or 6 blood oranges)

1 cup freshly squeezed orange juice (from about 3 oranges)

½ cup freshly squeezed lime juice (from about 4 limes)

½ cup Honey Syrup (page 160)

2 cups bourbon (try Woodford Reserve)

2 cups sparkling water

For Serving

Standard ice cubes, or floral ice cubes (see page 27)

1 (750 ml) bottle sparkling wine or brut Champagne, for topping

Citrus slices, for garnish

Edible flowers, for garnish

Make the ice ring: The day before the party, scatter the fresh citrus slices, mint leaves, and edible flowers around the bottom of a Bundt pan or other circular cake pan or jelly mold. Fill the pan halfway (to prevent overdilution of the punch) with filtered water, cover with plastic wrap, and place in the freezer for at least 12 hours.

Make the punch: In a punch bowl, combine the grapefruit juice, orange juice, lime juice, honey syrup, bourbon, and sparkling water.

Remove the Bundt mold from the freezer and dip the bottom into a bowl of warm water until the ice melts just enough to pop out of the mold. Place the ice ring in the punch bowl, rounded-side up.

To serve: Ladle the punch into double rocks glasses over ice. Top each glass with sparkling wine and garnish with a citrus slice and a bouquet of edible flowers.

winter spice sangria

To make a classic sangria, you can mix pretty much any bottle of red wine with 1 cup of brandy and ⅓ cup of simple syrup, then add the fruits of your choice. This is a hands-off, make-ahead pitcher of sangria that would be a splash at any fall or winter party. Set the pitcher out with plenty of ice and some club soda or sparkling water to add a bubbly finish to every glass.

1 (750 ml) bottle dry red wine, such as Grenache, Zinfandel, or Pinot Noir

½ cup orange liqueur

½ cup apple cider

¼ cup freshly squeezed orange juice

2 whole star anise

3 cinnamon sticks

1 whole clove

1 orange, cut into thin rounds

1 apple, cored and thinly sliced

1 pear, cored and thinly sliced

½ cup fresh pomegranate arils (optional)

2 cups standard ice cubes

Club soda or sparkling water

Optional garnishes: cinnamon sticks, orange rounds, apple slices, pear slices

In a large pitcher, combine the red wine, orange liqueur, apple cider, orange juice, star anise, cinnamon sticks, clove, orange rounds, apple slices, pear slices, and pomegranate arils (if using). Cover and refrigerate for at least 2 hours or up to 2 days.

To serve: Add some ice to the pitcher. Pour the sangria into glasses filled with ice and top with club soda or sparkling water. If desired, place a cinnamon stick and fruit in each glass to garnish.

120

Drinks for Cozy Occasions

There are plenty of drinks in this book that will inspire eating, dancing, and all-out celebrating. However, this chapter is dedicated to the drinks that instead encourage lingering around a dinner table and talking for hours, or settling into a comfortable chair by the fireplace for some evening reading (or scrolling, if we're being honest).

There's something for everyone here, whether you're in the mood for an after-dinner nightcap (try the Freezer Door Manhattan, page 129) or a drink in place of it (try the Après Ski Hot Chocolate, page 130). If you're looking for something boozy and on the rocks, try La Dolce Vita (page 125). Or if you're trying to create something impressive to pull out when the vibe is just right, consider a bottle of your very own bespoke Homemade Citrus-cello (page 138), making use of the season's best citrus and putting that bottle of Everclear to good use!

la dolce vita

This rum- and amaro-based drink is an ideal way to end the day with something sweet yet stiff and on the rocks. Scented with orange peel and gently spiced with bitters, it has all the gutsy personality of a classic old-fashioned or manhattan with some dessert-like luxury, too. This comes from the trifecta of molasses-y rum, caramelly Amaro Nonino, and one of my favorite liqueurs, Licor 43, a Spanish spirit that's made with vanilla, orange, and coriander. (See page 133 for another cocktail you can make with Licor 43.)

1½ ounces dark rum (try Diplomático Reserva)

¾ ounce Amaro Nonino

½ ounce Licor 43

½ ounce allspice dram (try St. Elizabeth) or spiced rum

4 or 5 dashes of cocoa bitters (try Scrappy's Bitters Chocolate)

Standard ice cubes, for mixing

1 large ice cube, for serving

Orange peel, for garnish

1 whole nutmeg, for grating (optional)

Place a rocks glass in the freezer.

In the chilled mixing glass, combine the rum, amaro, Licor 43, allspice dram, and bitters. Add a few ice cubes and stir swiftly with a barspoon for 20 seconds.

Strain into a chilled rocks glass over a large ice cube. "Swath" the glass with the orange peel by gently twisting it and running it all around the rim before adding it to the glass (see Do the Twist or Swath, page 28). Grate some nutmeg over the top, if desired.

pumpkin-spiced irish coffee

If you're already a pumpkin spice latte fan, you'll love this boozy spin on it. This cocktail borrows its structure from a classic Irish coffee—a comforting blend of hot coffee, booze, and cream. The autumnal twist comes from a mildly sweet pumpkin-spiced cold foam.

4 ounces hot freshly brewed dark roast coffee

1 teaspoon dark brown sugar

1½ ounces Irish whiskey (try blended whiskeys like Jameson, Tullamore D.E.W., or Bushmills here—you don't need to get too fancy)

¼ cup Pumpkin-Spiced Cream (recipe follows)

Ground cinnamon, for dusting

Pumpkin-Spiced Cream

1 cup half-and-half

1 tablespoon canned pumpkin puree

1 tablespoon maple syrup

½ teaspoon pumpkin pie spice

¼ teaspoon vanilla extract

In a mug, stir the hot coffee with the brown sugar until dissolved. Add the whiskey and stir. Dollop with pumpkin spiced cream and use a fine-mesh sieve to dust with ground cinnamon. Enjoy immediately.

Pumpkin-Spiced Cream

As a shortcut, you can also make this cream by combining 1 cup of half-and-half with 2 tablespoons of the Pumpkin Spice Syrup (page 162). This will keep in your fridge for up to 1 week, so make it to spoon onto hot cocoa, your regular morning cup of coffee, or even your next espresso martini.

MAKES A GENEROUS 1 CUP (9 OUNCES)

In a small bowl, combine the half-and-half, pumpkin puree, maple syrup, pumpkin pie spice, and vanilla. Using a handheld milk frother or whisk, agitate the cream until it is thick and thoroughly combined, 1 to 2 minutes. Use immediately or store in a sealed container for up to 1 week in the fridge. When ready to use, whisk (or use the frother) to revive the fluffy texture.

freezer door manhattan

When I have unexpected happy hour guests or guests who unexpectedly stay *very* late into the night, I'm reminded of the virtues of the freezer door cocktail—a prebatched, prediluted cocktail that happily lives in a bottle in my freezer door indefinitely. I usually make it when I have an empty bourbon bottle (I save them just to make these), but you could also use a new 750-milliliter bottle and just pour off 9½ ounces of the whiskey and reserve for another drink. Adding a tiny bit of water to the mix of bourbon, sweet vermouth (or try a split of dry and sweet vermouth), and bitters accounts for the subtle dilution you would normally achieve by shaking or stirring the drink with ice. All you need to do once guests roll in is divide the cocktail evenly among chilled glasses and top each one with a picture-perfect Maraschino cherry.

15 ounces bourbon or scotch (try Glenfiddich)

7 ounces sweet vermouth (try Carpano Antica)

2 ounces filtered water

½ ounce (or 18 dashes) aromatic bitters (I recommend trying a split of orange and aromatic bitters)

¼ ounce absinthe, to rinse the glass (optional)

Luxardo Maraschino cherries, for garnish

Using a funnel, add the whiskey, sweet vermouth, aromatic bitters, and water to a freezer-safe 750-milliliter bottle. (Alternatively omit the water and stir in a mixing glass with ice before serving for desired dilution.) Secure the cap tightly and shake lightly to mix. Place in your freezer to chill for at least 1 hour before serving.

When almost ready to serve, place 1 or more coupe glasses in the freezer to chill.

If using absinthe, rinse or spray the absinthe inside the chilled coupe glasses. (Learn more about this garnishing technique on page 28.) Pour 3 ounces of the cocktail into each glass and garnish with a Maraschino cherry.

après ski hot chocolate

I first fell in love with the combination of green Chartreuse and hot chocolate a few years ago when I was at a cousin's wedding in the French Alps (once in a lifetime experience, I'll tell you!). A local spot had it on the menu, and each sip warmed me from the inside out with its peppery, piney notes from the bitter liqueur. I think this cold-weather combination is enough reason to run out right now and buy a bottle of green Chartreuse if you don't already have it (I also call for this spirit in The Vacationer's Last Word, page 116). The mezcal is optional, but it adds an extra layer of smoky complexity. If you have a local bakery or sweets shop that happens to make especially good vanilla marshmallows, pick up a few to garnish each mug.

¼ cup unsweetened natural cocoa powder

¼ cup turbinado sugar or light brown sugar

3 cups whole milk

½ cup heavy cream

1 tablespoon vanilla extract

1 teaspoon ground cinnamon

Pinch of kosher salt

4 ounces green Chartreuse

2 ounces mezcal (optional; try Rey Campero)

Optional garnishes: Whipped cream, marshmallows, or ground cinnamon

In a medium saucepan, whisk together the cocoa powder, turbinado sugar, whole milk, heavy cream, vanilla, cinnamon, and kosher salt. Gently simmer over medium-low heat, whisking constantly, until the sugar has fully dissolved and the cocoa powder is fully combined, about 8 minutes (make sure you constantly whisk to avoid any burning or sticking to the bottom of the pan).

Once the mixture is steaming, divide it among four mugs and to each add 1 ounce Chartreuse and ½ ounce mezcal (if using). Stir to combine and garnish with whipped cream, marshmallows, and/or a dusting of cinnamon.

tiramisu espresso-tini

MAKES 1 COCKTAIL

Tiramisu and the espresso martini already have a whole lot in common—they're both sweet, boozy, and a pleasantly caffeinated way to end a meal. But this tiramisu espresso-tini goes a few steps further. It aims at complementing the espresso's nutty, toasted notes with a flash of chocolate liqueur.

1½ ounces vanilla vodka, store-bought or homemade (page 104)

1 ounce brewed espresso, cooled to room temperature (or cold brew concentrate)

¾ ounce coffee liqueur (try Mr Black)

½ ounce Licor 43

½ ounce chocolate liqueur (try Godiva)

Standard ice cubes, for shaking

2 tablespoons Mascarpone Cream (recipe follows)

Unsweetened cocoa powder, for dusting

3 espresso beans, for garnish

Mascarpone Cream

½ cup heavy cream

½ cup mascarpone, at room temperature

¼ cup powdered sugar

1 large egg yolk, at room temperature

1 teaspoon vanilla extract

Pinch of sea salt

Place a martini glass or coupe in the freezer to chill.

In a cocktail shaker, combine the vanilla vodka, espresso, coffee liqueur, Licor 43, and chocolate liqueur. Add ice, cover, and shake vigorously for 30 seconds.

Strain into your chilled glass. Top with mascarpone cream and gently use the back of the spoon to evenly flatten and smooth it if needed.

Using a small fine-mesh sieve, lightly dust cocoa powder across the surface (I like to coat about half of the surface for an asymmetrical look) and add the espresso beans on top. Serve immediately.

Mascarpone Cream

MAKES ABOUT 1½ CUPS (12 OUNCES)

In a medium bowl, combine the cream, mascarpone, powdered sugar, egg yolk, vanilla, and salt and whisk until the mixture has reached a rich, creamy consistency, about 5 minutes. Store in a sealed container in the refrigerator for up to 3 days.

lemon meringue martini

This frothy lemony cocktail is a tribute to my mom, whose favorite dessert is a lemon meringue pie. Since I prefer limoncello to lemon meringue, this cocktail is a happy midpoint between our tastes—finally a way for us to enjoy her favorite dessert together. The egg white softens the tartness of the lemon, and the brûléed lemon wheel adds just a touch of that burnt sugar you'd get from browning the meringue topping. This is a great way to use your homemade limoncello (see Homemade Citrus-cello, page 138) and transport yourself to the Amalfi coast.

Brûléed lemon garnish: 1 lemon wheel (sliced ¼ inch thick) and ½ teaspoon granulated sugar

1 ounce vanilla vodka, store-bought or homemade (page 104)

¾ ounce heavy cream

¾ ounce limoncello, store-bought or homemade (page 138)

¾ ounce freshly squeezed lemon juice

¾ ounce amaretto (try Disaronno)

1 large egg white or 2 tablespoons aquafaba

½ ounce Plain Simple Syrup (page 160)

Standard ice cubes, for shaking

Place a coupe or small stemmed glass of your choice in the freezer to chill.

For the brûléed lemon garnish: Set the lemon wheel on a sheet pan and sprinkle the sugar across the surface of it. Use a handheld torch (or your broiler) to brûlé the sugar until it turns golden brown and the sugar starts to bubble. Set the garnish aside.

In a cocktail shaker, combine the vanilla vodka, heavy cream, limoncello, lemon juice, amaretto, egg white (make sure that there are no bits of yolk; the fat will prevent the white from getting frothy), and simple syrup. Cover and dry shake (without ice) vigorously for 20 seconds to froth the egg white (or use a hand frother if you have one).

Add the ice and continue shaking vigorously for an additional 30 seconds. Double-strain into the chilled glass and top with the brûléed lemon slice, sugar-side up.

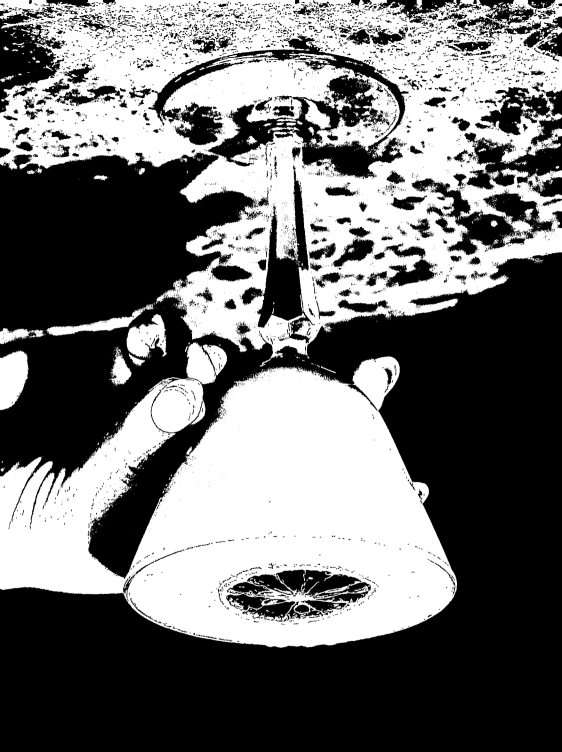

nonna's tom & jerry

Similar to eggnog but served warm with a whipped silky texture, this recipe has been in my family since the 1940s. Warm, custardy, and full of cinnamon and nutmeg, this will win over any eggnog fans in a heartbeat.

¼ cup Tom & Jerry Base (recipe follows)

2 ounces dark rum (try Appleton Estate or The Real McCoy), brandy (try De Luze Cognac), or 1 ounce of each

4 ounces hot water

1 whole nutmeg, for grating

1 whole star anise, for garnish

1 cinnamon stick, for garnish

Tom & Jerry Base

6 large eggs, separated, at room temperature

1 teaspoon cream of tartar

4 cups powdered sugar

2 teaspoons vanilla extract

1 teaspoon freshly grated nutmeg

½ teaspoon ground cinnamon, plus more to taste

Scoop the Tom & Jerry base into a mug or handled cup—most Tom & Jerry sets (see Note) come with matching handled cups. Stir in the rum and hot water. Grate fresh nutmeg on top and place a star anise pod and a cinnamon stick on top.

Tom & Jerry Base

MAKES ENOUGH FOR 12 DRINKS

In a stand mixer bowl fitted with the whisk attachment, combine the egg whites and cream of tartar (or use a large bowl and a hand mixer). Whip on low speed until combined, then increase to medium and beat the egg whites until foamy, about 5 minutes. With the mixer on medium, slowly add 2 cups of the powdered sugar. Increase the mixer speed to medium-high, beating until the egg whites form stiff peaks, about 5 minutes. Transfer to a large bowl.

Clean the bowl and add the egg yolks. Start on low speed and gradually whisk in the remaining 2 cups powdered sugar, followed by the vanilla, nutmeg, and cinnamon, mixing until silky and it has a beige hue.

Pour this yolk mixture into a Tom & Jerry bowl or holiday serving bowl. Using a rubber spatula, gently fold the meringue into the yolk mixture until fully incorporated and there are no streaks.

Cover and refrigerate until you're ready to serve. You can make the base up to 3 days before serving.

homemade citrus-cello

MAKES ABOUT 3 CUPS (24 OUNCES)

Homemade limoncello may sound like it involves some serious craftsmanship, but it's mostly just a waiting game as you let the essence of the citrus peels infuse in the alcohol over the course of a few weeks. My mom loves drizzling Homemade Citrus-cello over ice cream along with a little olive oil and lemon zest. It's also key in my Lemon Meringue Martini (page 134).

About 2 pounds organic large lemons or Meyer lemons (about 10), blood oranges, and/or navel oranges, or citrus of choice

1 (750 ml) bottle Everclear or vodka (try Grey Goose)

½ cup Plain Simple Syrup (page 160), plus more to taste

Wash the citrus well to help remove any waxy residue and pat them completely dry. Using a Y-peeler, peel off the zest in strips, avoiding the bitter white pith. (If a significant amount of pith remains on the strips, lay the strip pith-side up and carefully trim it away using a paring knife.) Juice 1 of the lemons. (Save the rest of the peeled lemons in the fridge to juice for another use; see Note.)

Add the lemon zest, lemon juice, and Everclear to a 32-ounce jar or bottle, cover, and shake. Place in a dark, cool area and gently shake at least once a week for 4 weeks to redistribute the zest.

To serve, strain the mixture through a cheesecloth-lined fine-mesh sieve and into a large bowl; discard the lemon zest. Add the simple syrup, taste, and add more until you've reached your desired sweetness. Use a funnel to transfer the citrus-cello into a bottle or large jar.

Cover tightly and let the finished citrus-cello sit at room temperature for 7 days to allow the flavors to mellow. At this point, move the sealed jar or bottle to the freezer and store for up to 1 year.

Booze-Free Beauties

As much as I love my collection of bourbons and tequilas, there are times when I'm in the mood for all the flavor with none of the alcohol. If you're not drinking—for any reason—you still deserve the joy of kick-starting the party or relaxing into the weekend with a fun nonalcoholic drink.

This chapter is full of sometimes fruity, sometimes herbal, always celebratory drinks that will make anyone feel pampered. There's a juniper-infused, gin-less tonic on page 148 and a spritz that's full of rhubarb and orange nuance on page 144. Whether you've built out a collection of nonalcoholic alternatives to common spirits or not, this chapter will give you plenty of ideas for how to hold the booze and party on.

orange dreamsicle

This nonalcoholic drink hits all the sweet, creamy, citrusy notes of an orange Creamsicle but has a lot more nuance than its frozen dessert counterpart. The coconut milk and vanilla syrup's mellow sweetness and silky richness rival the best vanilla ice cream you've ever had. And homemade orange soda (as simple as stirring together some fresh orange juice, club soda, and a quick infused syrup) levels up the fresh fruit flavors.

2 ounces canned unsweetened coconut milk (try Thai Kitchen)

3 ounces freshly squeezed orange juice

½ ounce Vanilla Syrup (page 163)

Standard ice cubes, for shaking and for serving

2 ounces orange soda, homemade (recipe follows) or a good-quality store-bought brand (such as Olipop or Poppi), for topping

Fresh thinly sliced orange wheel, for garnish

Orange Soda

3 cups club soda

1 cup freshly squeezed orange juice

½ ounce Orange Zest Syrup (page 164), plus more to taste

In a cocktail shaker, combine the coconut milk, orange juice, and vanilla syrup. Add ice, cover, and shake vigorously for 30 seconds. Double-strain into a double rocks glass filled with ice and top with the orange soda. Place a fresh orange wheel in the glass.

Orange Soda

MAKES 4 CUPS (32 OUNCES)

In a large pitcher, combine the club soda, orange juice, and orange zest syrup and stir to combine. Add more syrup to taste if needed.

free spirit spritz

In my world, everyone deserves a spritz, whether they drink alcohol or not. This is why I set out to reconstruct some of my favorite flavors (and the bright hue) of Aperol— minus the Aperol. The beloved aperitif has a distinctly bitter flavor, with notes of rhubarb, gentian (a bitter and herbal flavor), and other botanicals. Here, I achieve the balance with a tart rhubarb shrub, some fresh orange juice, bittersweet homemade cranberry syrup, and the slightly peppery quinine flavor of tonic water.

2 ounces Rhubarb Shrub (page 167)

1 ounce freshly squeezed orange juice

½ ounce Cranberry Syrup (page 166)

2 ounces tonic water

Standard ice cubes, for serving

Fresh orange wedge, for garnish

In a large wine glass or double rocks glass, combine the rhubarb shrub, orange juice, and cranberry syrup. Add ice and stir. Top with tonic water and stir again. Place a fresh orange wheel in the glass.

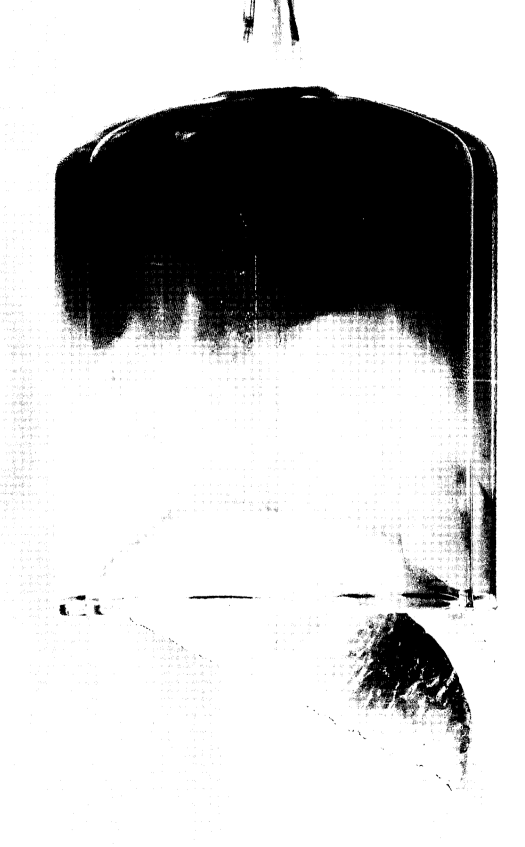

booze-free margarita

A margarita can be so many things, but what I find important is the scent of salt and fresh lime juice that hits your nose before the first sip, the gentle agave sweetness, and even the feeling of the weighty, icy glass in your hand. I firmly believe that everyone deserves a margarita, with tequila or not! Plus, the world of nonalcoholic spirits is rapidly changing and expanding, and every time I taste a new tequila alternative, I'm stunned by how subtlely each flavor is re-created. But even if you skip that 1-ounce addition altogether, you'll still have a balanced, vibrantly citrusy drink to sip on all night.

For the rim: lime wedge and kosher salt or chile salt

1 ounce freshly squeezed lime juice

¾ ounce freshly squeezed orange juice

½ ounce agave syrup

1 ounce tequila alternative, such as Ritual Zero Proof Tequila or Seedlip (optional)

Standard ice cubes, for shaking and serving

Citrus-flavored sparkling water, such as grapefruit Topo Chico or lime Spindrift, for topping

Dehydrated citrus wheel (see Dehydrate Those Slices, page 29), for garnish

Run the lime wedge around the outer rim of a margarita or rocks glass and roll the rim in the salt or chile salt (see A Rimmed Glass, page 28). Place the rimmed glass in the freezer to chill.

In a cocktail shaker, combine the lime juice, orange juice, agave, and tequila alternative (if using). Add ice, cover, and shake vigorously for 30 seconds. Double-strain into the chilled glass. Top with sparkling water and place a dehydrated citrus wheel on top.

minus
the gin & tonic

This nonalcoholic version is inspired by the Spanish approach to gin and tonics—herbaceous, maximalist, and packed with bright juniper flavor. Below, you'll find two options for replacing the juniper-scented, botanical flavor of the gin: One uses a nonalcoholic gin alternative and the other uses juniper berry tea, which can easily be found online. Some brands' tea bags even contain whole juniper berries, which double as a garnish here.

2 ounces nonalcoholic gin alternative, such as Monday Zero Alcohol Gin

4 ounces tonic water

Standard ice cubes, for serving

Optional garnishes: 1 fresh lime wheel, 2 or 3 cucumber slices, 1 or 2 fresh basil sprigs, 4 or 5 black peppercorns, and/or 2 or 3 juniper berries

Minus the Gin Alternative

8 ounces brewed juniper berry tea, such as Tazo, cooled to room temperature

2 ounces Cucumber Syrup (page 165)

12 ounces tonic water, for topping each drink

Standard ice cubes, for serving

Optional garnishes: 1 fresh lime wheel, 2 or 3 cucumber slices, 1 or 2 fresh basil sprigs, 4 or 5 black peppercorns, and/or 2 or 3 juniper berries

In a large wine glass or balloon glass, combine the gin alternative, tonic water, and ice. Stir and garnish with the lime wheel, cucumber slice, sprig of basil, black peppercorns, and/or juniper berries.

Minus the Gin Alternative

MAKES 4 MOCKTAILS

In a pitcher, stir together the tea, cucumber syrup, and tonic water. Add ice to four individual wine glasses and divide the mixture evenly among them. Stir together and garnish with the fresh lime wheel, cucumber slices, sprig of basil, black peppercorns, and/or juniper berries.

148

melon no-jito

This melon-based nonalcoholic cocktail has all the elements of a great mojito but none of the booze. There's fresh lime juice, plenty of mint, and a touch of sweetness from simple syrup. I am melon agnostic, so use what you like—watermelon offers a thirst-quenching quality, while cantaloupe brings mild, floral notes. No need for a fancy juicer either—use my blend-and-strain trick to turn that melon into mocktail material in seconds flat.

1 ounce freshly squeezed lime juice

4 fresh mint leaves, plus more for garnish

½ ounce Plain Simple Syrup (page 160)

Pinch of sea salt

3 ounces Melon Juice (recipe follows)

2 to 3 ounces sparkling water, for topping

Standard ice cubes, for shaking and serving

Fresh lime wedge, for garnish

Melon Juice

1 cup fresh melon chunks

¼ cup cold filtered water

Place a double rocks or highball glass in the freezer to chill.

In a cocktail shaker, muddle together the lime juice, mint leaves, simple syrup, and sea salt. Add the melon juice and ice, cover, and shake vigorously for 30 seconds.

Fill the chilled glass with ice and double-strain the contents of the cocktail shaker into the glass. Top with sparkling water, add a fresh lime wedge on top, and gently slap fresh mint in hand (see Smack the Mint, page 36) and place it in the glass.

Melon Juice

MAKES ABOUT 1 CUP (ABOUT 8 OUNCES)

In a blender, combine the melon chunks and water and blend on medium-high speed until smooth with no visible chunks, 1 to 2 minutes. Strain through a fine-mesh sieve into a sealable container. Cover and refrigerate until ready to use. The juice can be made up to 3 days in advance.

nonalcoholic carajillo

Carajillo translates to "courage" in Spanish, and variations of the drink generally involve the 1:1 punch of a shot of espresso and a shot of brandy or rum—or Licor 43, in the case of my favorite style. This tribute to the drink is full of caffeinated courage, minus the alcohol. Since we're skipping the Licor 43, which has a soft vanilla-citrus aroma, this iced carajillo gets a squeeze of fresh orange juice and a complex sweetness from a vanilla-cinnamon simple syrup.

2 ounces freshly brewed espresso, cooled

¾ ounce Vanilla & Cinnamon Syrup (page 163)

½ ounce freshly squeezed orange juice

Standard ice cubes, for shaking

1 large ice cube, for serving

Orange twist (see Do the Twist or Swath, page 28) or freshly grated orange zest, for garnish

Cinnamon stick, for grating

In a cocktail shaker, combine the espresso, syrup, and orange juice. Add ice, cover, and shake vigorously for 30 seconds. Double-strain into a rocks glass over a large ice cube. Add a fresh orange twist or zest and grate some cinnamon across the surface of the drink.

tiki tiki tiki room

The mix of delicately sweet coconut water, fresh pineapple, and bracingly sour grapefruit juice give this drink a whole lot of character and sunshine with zero chances of a hangover. In fact, this tropical-inspired cocktail is proof (or should I say "zero-proof") that, despite what the beer commercials might have you believe, you definitely don't need alcohol to be transported to the beachy vacation mode. (But if you miss the trademark tiki flavor of rum, try adding an ounce of a rum alternative, like the one made by Lyre's.)

Standard ice cubes, for serving

4 ounces coconut water

3 ounces Fresh Pineapple Juice (page 82)

1 ounce freshly squeezed grapefruit juice

2 ounces sparkling water, for topping

Grapefruit wedges, for garnish

Fill a wine glass or double rocks glass with standard ice cubes. Add the coconut water, pineapple juice, and grapefruit juice and give it a stir. Top with sparkling water and place a grapefruit wedges on top.

garden refresher punch

I take pride in welcoming guests as if they were entering a five-star hotel. That's why this punch has serious spa vibes. It's almost as if you walked into your garden (fictional or real), grabbed all the freshest ingredients you could find, and turned them into a cooling, bubbly tonic. The cucumbers, which I like to blend skin-on, give this a beautiful pale green tint that creates a stunning contrast to the lavender garnish. If you have a gin alternative (I like the ones from Ritual Zero Proof and Monday), feel free to add a splash to this.

2 cups Cucumber Juice (recipe follows)

½ ounce lavender simple syrup (see Herbaceous Syrups, page 162)

2 cups tonic water, or to taste

¾ cup freshly squeezed lime juice (from about 6 large limes)

3 cups standard ice cubes for the pitcher, plus more for individual glasses

Fresh lime wheels, lavender sprigs, and/or violas, for garnish

Cucumber Juice

4 Persian (mini) cucumbers, sliced about ½ inch thick (about 5 cups)

1 cup cold filtered water

In a large pitcher, combine the cucumber juice, lavender syrup, fresh lime juice, and tonic water. Add the ice and stir. Add fresh lime wheels, lavender sprigs, and/or fresh violas to the pitcher.

For each glass, add ice cubes and fill with the mocktail mixture. Place a fresh lime wheel and fresh lavender sprig in each glass.

Cucumber Juice

MAKES ABOUT 2½ CUPS (ABOUT 20 OUNCES)

In a blender, combine the cucumbers and water and blend on medium-high speed until smooth, 1 to 2 minutes. Strain through a fine-mesh sieve into a medium bowl or measuring cup. Transfer to a sealed container and refrigerate. It will keep for up to 7 days.

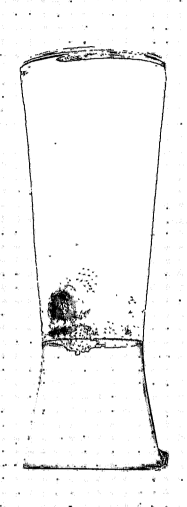

Pretty Simples and Shrubs

Simple syrups are a key part of any bartender's tool kit. And lucky for home bartenders like us, this building block of cocktail making is as easy as melting sugar into water.

While regular granulated sugar is really the only ingredient you need to make a simple syrup or a shrub, you can also get creative by using sweeteners like honey, brown sugar, demerara sugar, or even monk fruit sugar, each of which adds its unique taste.

Syrups are an easy way to bring your drinks to life with the flavors, aromas, and colors of your favorite seasonal fruits, flowers, herbs, and spices.

Shrubs are drinking vinegars that are not only a great way to preserve fresh seasonal produce, but they can also add a new level of sweet acidity to your cocktails.

And let's not forget about infusions, from homemade chile liqueur to vanilla vodka. Once you start making your own infusions at home, it's hard to stop!

plain simple syrup

MAKES ABOUT 1½ CUPS (12 OUNCES)

A 1:1 sugar-to-water ratio gives you a syrup that's fluid enough to incorporate quickly into cocktails with just a few quick stirs or shakes, and one that also has a level of sweetness that's easy to control and tweak as needed. Some drinks call for a "rich syrup," in which the sugar is doubled for a syrup that's even thicker and sweeter than the standard plain syrup here.

1 cup granulated sugar

1 cup filtered water

In a saucepan, combine the sugar and water and bring to a simmer over medium heat, stirring occasionally, until the sugar has completely dissolved, 3 to 5 minutes.

Remove from the heat and let cool in the saucepan to room temperature, or for quick cooling, pour into a heatproof container and throw in the freezer for up to 5 minutes. Funnel and store in a sealed container or funnel into a squeeze bottle and refrigerate up to 1 month (if it becomes cloudy or you see mold on the surface, toss it and make a new batch).

 For a quick simple syrup, pour 1 cup hot water over 1 cup sugar in a heatproof jar or bottle and mix to dissolve completely.

For a quick vanilla simple syrup, stir in 1 tablespoon of vanilla extract before storing.

honey syrup

MAKES ABOUT 1½ CUPS (12 OUNCES)

If you've ever tried to stir honey into a glass of iced tea, you know that the dense substance has a tendency to sink to the bottom of the glass. Simmering honey briefly with an equal volume of water makes it far easier to shake or stir into cold drinks, and it allows you to control and fine-tune the sweetness. Use a honey syrup in cocktails like the Kumquat Kick (page 52) or The Weekenders' Party Punch (page 119).

1 cup mild honey (try a local honey or an acacia honey)

1 cup filtered water

In a medium saucepan, combine the honey and water and bring to a simmer over medium heat, stirring occasionally, until the honey is completely dispersed.

Remove from the heat and cool to room temperature. Funnel it into in a sealed container or syrup bottle, and store in the refrigerator for up to 1 month.

DIFFERENT HONEYS AND THEIR FLAVORS

Acacia, clover, or wildflower honey: This is a sweet yet classic honey flavor, perfect for a classic Bee's Knees cocktail!

Eucalyptus honey: This adds flavors of menthol, caramel, and earthiness, perfect for tea-based cocktails or to add to your next London Fog!

Buckwheat honey: Use this for flavors of rich molasses and toffee, perfect for a hot toddy!

Orange blossom honey: This has floral and citrus flavors, perfect for a Gold Rush or as a sweetener for a whiskey sour!

strawberry syrup

MAKES ABOUT 1½ CUPS (12 OUNCES)

This is a dramatically beautiful way to add a pop of pink to your drink, and it lets you preserve that fresh strawberry flavor in the weeks after you've picked up your farmers' market haul. After straining the syrup, use the sweetened strawberries as a breakfast topping or on your next ice cream sundae. Use in The Pink Daiquiri (page 47) or the Rhubarb & Cognac Fizz (page 40).

1 cup granulated sugar

8 to 10 small strawberries, hulled and roughly chopped (1 cup)

1 cup filtered water

In a saucepan, combine the sugar, strawberries, and water and bring to a simmer over medium heat, stirring occasionally until the sugar has completely dissolved, about 5 minutes.

Reduce to a simmer and continue to cook until the syrup has thickened slightly and turned a rich red color, about 10 minutes.

Remove from the heat and let cool completely. Strain through a sieve into a liquid measuring cup (save the strawberries for another use.) Funnel it into an airtight container or syrup bottle and store in the refrigerator for up to 1 month.

cherry syrup

MAKES ABOUT 1½ CUPS (12 OUNCES)

Keeping this syrup in your fridge means that you're only moments away from your next DIY cherry cola or cherry lemonade. Use your favorite local, seasonal variety of cherry if you can (yes, even sour cherries!), but the bags of pitted cherries in the freezer aisle work, too. For a sweet, nostalgic spin, add 1 teaspoon vanilla extract after straining.

1 cup granulated sugar

1 cup pitted fresh (such as Bing or Rainier) or frozen cherries

1 cup filtered water

In a saucepan, combine the sugar, cherries, and water and bring to a simmer over medium heat, stirring occasionally until the sugar has completely dissolved, about 5 minutes.

Reduce to a simmer and cook until cherries soften and cook down to a deep red color and are slightly thickened, about 10 minutes.

Remove from the heat and let cool completely. Strain through a sieve into a liquid measuring cup, pressing against the cherries with the back of a silicone spatula to extract all the syrup. (Save the cherries for another use, like topping vanilla ice cream.) Funnel it into an airtight container or syrup bottle and store in the refrigerator for up to 1 month.

herbaceous syrups

MAKES ABOUT 1½ CUPS (12 OUNCES)

Most fresh herbs are prime for infusing simple syrup for a cocktail. Basil brings bright, fresh, green power to the Bourbon & Basil Smash (page 39), Apricot French 75 (page 103), or Stone Fruit Whiskey Sour (page 112). Lavender is packed with springtime aromas and gives a lush scent. Use this in the Garden Refresher Punch (page 156) or cup of tea or lemonade. Thyme pairs especially well with floral-driven and gin-forward drinks like a gin and tonic. Citrus Party Punch Spritz (page 74) or Blood Orange Thyme Margaritas (page 93). Rosemary's piney wintery flavor goes so well with bitter Campari in a Smoked Rosemary Negroni Sour (page 108).

1 cup granulated sugar

Herb of choice: 8 medium basil leaves or 2 tablespoons food-grade dried lavender flowers (or fresh lavender flower blossoms) or 8 thyme sprigs, or 5 rosemary sprigs

1 cup filtered water

In a saucepan, combine the sugar, herb, and water and bring to a simmer over medium heat, stirring occasionally until the sugar has completely dissolved.

Reduce to a simmer to allow the flavors to infuse and simmer until the syrup is tinted slightly to reflect the color of the herb, about 10 minutes.

Remove from the heat and let cool to room temperature. Strain through a fine-mesh sieve into a measuring cup, pressing against the herbs with the back of a silicone spatula to extract all the syrup. Funnel it into an airtight container or syrup bottle and store in the refrigerator for up to 1 month.

pumpkin spice syrup

MAKES ABOUT 1½ CUPS (12 OUNCES)

Anyone who thinks they don't like pumpkin spice lattes has probably only had versions made with syrup that's packed with artificial flavors and corn syrup. But when you make this barista and bartender staple at home, you can sweeten it with brown sugar, vanilla, and real cinnamon sticks. Use this in the Pumpkin-Spiced Irish Coffee (page 126) or try it in your next rum-based old-fashioned.

1 cup packed light brown sugar

¼ cup canned unsweetened pumpkin puree (try Farmers Market Organic)

1 tablespoon pumpkin pie spice

1 cup filtered water

2 cinnamon sticks

2 teaspoons vanilla extract

In a saucepan, combine the brown sugar, pumpkin puree, pumpkin pie spice, and water and bring to a simmer over medium heat, stirring occasionally until the sugar has completely dissolved, about 2 minutes.

Reduce to a simmer and continue cooking until the syrup has thickened slightly and turned to a deeper orange hue, about 10 minutes.

Remove from the heat and let cool completely. Strain through a fine-mesh sieve into a measuring cup and stir in the vanilla. Funnel it into an airtight container or syrup bottle and store in the refrigerator for up to 1 month.

cinnamon syrup

MAKES ABOUT 1½ CUPS (12 OUNCES)

I love simmering whole cinnamon sticks in simple syrup. The syrup is the perfect balance between sweet and fragrant.

1 cup packed light brown sugar

4 cinnamon sticks

1 cup filtered water

In a saucepan, combine the brown sugar, cinnamon sticks, and water and bring to a simmer over medium heat, stirring occasionally until the sugar has completely dissolved, about 5 minutes.

Reduce to a simmer and continue to cook until the syrup has thickened slightly and turns light brown, about 10 minutes.

Remove from the heat and let cool completely. Strain through a sieve into a measuring cup and discard the cinnamon sticks. Funnel it into an airtight container or syrup bottle and store in the refrigerator for up to 1 month.

Vanilla & Cinnamon Syrup: Add 1 halved and scraped vanilla bean to the pan with the cinnamon sticks and proceed with recipe. Or, make the recipe for Cinnamon Syrup as-is and add 1½ teaspoons vanilla bean paste or 1 tablespoon vanilla extract after removing the syrup from the heat.

vanilla syrup

MAKES ABOUT 1½ CUPS (12 OUNCES)

Try this syrup in the Passion Fruit Martini (page 104) or the Orange Dreamsicle (page 143).

1 cup granulated sugar

1 cup filtered water

1 soft and supple vanilla bean or
½ tablespoon vanilla bean paste

In a medium saucepan, combine the sugar and water. If using the vanilla bean, slice the vanilla bean in half lengthwise and use a paring knife to scrape the seeds into the pan, then add the scraped vanilla pod as well. Otherwise, just stir in vanilla bean paste after the syrup is made and cooled.

Bring to a simmer over medium heat, stirring occasionally, until the sugar has completely dissolved, about 5 minutes.

Remove from the heat and let cool completely. Strain through a mesh sieve into a measuring cup. Funnel it into an airtight container or syrup bottle and store in the refrigerator for up to 1 month.

orange zest syrup

MAKES ABOUT 1½ CUPS (12 OUNCES)

In addition to trying this in the nonalcoholic Orange Dreamsicle (page 143), you can try this one in your next old-fashioned or whiskey sour.

1 cup granulated sugar

Zest of 1 large orange, freshly grated

1 cup filtered water

In a saucepan, combine the sugar, orange zest, and water and bring to a simmer over medium heat, stirring occasionally until the sugar has completely dissolved, about 5 minutes.

Reduce to a simmer and continue to cook until the syrup has thickened slightly and is lightly tinted orange, about 10 minutes.

Remove from the heat and let cool completely. Strain through a fine-mesh sieve in a measuring cup. Funnel it into an airtight container or syrup bottle and store in the refrigerator for up to 1 month.

prosecco syrup

MAKES ABOUT 1½ CUPS (12 OUNCES)

Do you ever have an unfinished half bottle of prosecco lying around after a party? Me neither. But hey—it *could* happen, and that's when you'll make this fruity-tart syrup. Give it a go in Rosé All Day Spritz Punch (page 73).

1 cup prosecco

1 cup granulated sugar

In a saucepan, combine the prosecco and sugar and bring to a simmer over medium heat, stirring occasionally until the sugar has completely dissolved, about 5 minutes.

Remove from the heat and let cool completely. Funnel it into an airtight container or syrup bottle and store in the refrigerator for up to 1 month.

cucumber syrup

MAKES ABOUT 1½ CUPS (12 OUNCES)

Cucumber Syrup wonders in the booze-free Minus the Gin & Tonic (page 148), you should also try it in your next classic gin and tonic, too. Try adding a few fresh mint leaves or a sprig of rosemary along with the cucumber.

1 cup granulated sugar

1 cup chopped Persian (mini) or
English cucumber

1 cup filtered water

In a saucepan, combine the sugar, cucumber, and water and bring to a simmer over medium heat, stirring occasionally until the sugar has completely dissolved.

Reduce to a simmer and continue to cook until the syrup has thickened slightly and the cucumbers have softened, about 20 minutes.

Remove from the heat and let cool completely. Strain through a sieve into a measuring cup. Funnel into an airtight container or syrup bottle and store in the refrigerator for up to 1 month.

persimmon syrup

MAKES ABOUT 1½ CUPS (12 OUNCES)

Persimmons have such a fleeting season (late autumn through early winter) that I always find myself hoarding them when they're at their best and turning them into as many cocktail ingredients as possible, like the persimmon puree and syrup used in the Persimmon Mezcal Sour (page 115). I prefer sweet Fuyu persimmons (doughnut shaped), which are firmer when ripe, or Hachiya persimmons (acorn shaped), which will only be sweet when ripe and soft to the touch. Try adding a few cinnamon sticks while simmering.

1 cup turbinado sugar or packed light
brown sugar

1 cup roughly chopped Fuyu persimmons
(about 2 persimmons)

1 cup filtered water

In a saucepan, combine the sugar, persimmons, and water and bring to a simmer over medium heat, stirring occasionally until the sugar has completely dissolved, about 5 minutes.

Reduce to a simmer and continue to cook until the syrup has thickened slightly and turns a light orange, about 20 minutes.

Remove from the heat and let cool completely. Strain through a fine-mesh sieve into a measuring cup. Funnel it into an airtight container or syrup bottle and store in the refrigerator for up to 1 month.

spicy pepper syrup

MAKES ABOUT 1½ CUPS (12 OUNCES)

This zippy syrup adds warmth to the cool and creamy Avocado Margarita (page 85). Jalapeños' heat level can vary quite a bit from pepper to pepper. I recommend tasting a piece raw, which will help you gauge whether to add ¼ cup of slices or a full ½ cup. Habaneros are even spicier than jalapeños, so taste as you go and adjust quantities as needed. This fiery syrup is a great match for smoky mezcal in the Pineapple Mezcal Margarita (page 82).

1 cup granulated sugar

1 to 2 jalapeños, thinly sliced into rings (¼ to ½ cup depending on your heat tolerance) or 1 to 2 habanero peppers (depending on your spice preference), seeded and thinly sliced into rings

1 cup filtered water

In a saucepan, combine the sugar, chile peppers, and water and bring to a simmer over medium heat, stirring occasionally until the sugar has completely dissolved, about 5 minutes.

Reduce to a simmer and continue to cook until the syrup has thickened slightly, 8 to 10 minutes.

Remove from the heat. At this point, taste your syrup. If it's on the spicy side, strain the syrup now. If it could bear to be a little spicier, leave the jalapeños or habaneros in the syrup to steep while it cools to room temperature.

Strain through a fine-mesh sieve into a measuring cup. Funnel it into an airtight container or syrup bottle and store in the refrigerator for up to 1 month.

cranberry syrup

MAKES ABOUT 1½ CUPS (12 OUNCES)

Because of their bitter-tart punch and vibrant red color, cranberries have a lot of cocktail potential, especially in booze-free drinks like the Free Spirit Spritz (page 144), where they hit some of the sultry notes that usually fall to the bitter aperitifs on the bar cart.

1 cup granulated sugar

1 cup fresh or frozen cranberries

1 cup filtered water

In a saucepan, combine the sugar, cranberries, and water and bring to a simmer over medium heat, stirring occasionally until the sugar has completely dissolved, about 5 minutes.

Reduce to a simmer and continue to cook until the cranberries begin to pop, about 10 minutes.

Remove from the heat and let cool to room temperature. Strain through a sieve into a measuring cup, using a spatula to press down on the berries to release all the juices, and discard the cranberries or reserve them for a dessert topping. Funnel the syrup into an airtight container or syrup bottle and store in the refrigerator for up to 1 month.

Cranberry Juice Syrup: Instead of using fresh or frozen cranberries, add 1 cup unsweetened cranberry juice to the saucepan with the sugar (don't add water). Simmer and cool as instructed.

rhubarb shrub

MAKES ABOUT 1½ CUPS (12 OUNCES)

Think of a shrub as a drinking vinegar. It's a nonalcoholic syrup that can be easily paired with a little sparkling water or used as a sweet yet acidic addition in cocktails. It's made by combining fruits, herbs, and/or spices with sugar and vinegar and then allowing the mixture to infuse over a period of time, about 5 days total. Shrubs can have loads of flavor combinations in addition to rhubarb, try plum-rosemary or even cucumber-thyme. Due to the acidity the shrub will have, it's important to create balance in a cocktail, which may mean backing down on the fresh citrus ingredients in a recipe. Try in the Rhubarb & Cognac Fizz (page 40) or the Free Spirit Spritz (page 144).

2 cups finely chopped rhubarb (about 2 rhubarb stalks) or your favorite seasonal ingredient, such as strawberries, or pineapple

1 cup granulated sugar

1 cup apple cider vinegar

In a lidded container, combine the rhubarb and sugar and let sit for 24 hours to macerate.

The next day, add the vinegar to the shrub and mix to combine. Let sit for 3 to 4 days, mixing occasionally, until the sugar fully dissolves.

Strain the shrub into a measuring cup and then funnel it into a covered jar or bottle and store in the refrigerator for up to 6 weeks.

chile liqueur

MAKES ABOUT 2 CUPS (16 OUNCES)

A spicy liqueur is a bar cart staple for me, which, judging by the recipes in the book, shouldn't take you by surprise. You can use chile liqueur in loads of cocktails in the margarita chapter or in recipes like Kumquat Kick (page 52). The dried chiles can be purchases or dried at home in a dehydrator or low oven.

1 or 2 ancho chiles or other dried chile of choice

1½ cups vodka (try Harridan)

¾ cup Plain Simple Syrup (page 160)

Remove the seeds of the dried chiles (or leave in a few seeds if you love lots of heat!). Place them in a 36-ounce jar and add the vodka. Cover tightly and let infuse for about 2 weeks, giving it a light shake every other day.

Once at the desired heat level, strain the vodka through a sieve into a measuring cup. Stir in rich simple syrup and mix to combine. Funnel the mixture back into the 36-ounce jar or an empty vodka bottle and store in a cool dark place, where it will last indefinitely.

 If you're into infusions, be sure to check out the strawberry-infused Aperol on page 81, the olive oil–infused gin on page 100, and the vanilla-infused vodka on page 104.

Don't let that simple syrup go to waste, here are some simple three-ingredient cocktail combinations to ensure you're using those syrups to the fullest.

LAVENDER GIN & TONIC

½ ounce lavender syrup (see Herbaceous Syrups, page 162) + 2 ounces gin + 4 ounces tonic

ORANGE ZEST CUBA LIBRE

½ ounce Orange Zest Syrup (page 164) + 2 ounces dark rum + 4 ounces cola

GOLD RUSH

½ ounce Honey Syrup (page 160) + ¾ ounce lemon juice + 2 ounces bourbon

STRAWBERRY SHRUB SODA

½ ounce Strawberry Syrup (page 161) + ¾ ounce Rhubarb Shrub (page 167) + 4 ounces club soda

CRANBERRY VODKA SODA

½ ounce Cranberry Syrup (page 166) + 1½ ounces vodka + 4 ounces club soda

HERBACEOUS BEE'S KNEES

½ ounce Herbaceous Syrup (page 162, made with herb of choice) + ¾ ounce lemon juice + 2 ounces gin

PUMPKIN PIE ICE LATTE

½ ounce Pumpkin Pie Spice Syrup (page 162) + 1 to 2 ounces milk + 5 ounces cold brew

CINNAMON OLD-FASHIONED

½ ounce Cinnamon Syrup (page 163) + 2 to 3 dashes of bitters + 2 ounces bourbon

SPICY GREYHOUND

½ ounce Spicy Pepper Syrup (page 166) + 1½ ounces gin + 3 ounces grapefruit juice

SPIKED VANILLA COLA

½ ounce Vanilla Syrup (page 163) + 2 ounces bourbon + 4 ounces cola

CUCUMBER GIMLET

½ ounce Cucumber Syrup (page 165) + ¾ ounce lime juice + 2 ounces gin

CHERRY SUNRISE

½ ounce Cherry Syrup (page 161) + 1½ ounces tequila + 4 ounces orange juice

PERSIMMON COLLINS

¾ ounce Persimmon Syrup (page 165) + 1 ounce lemon juice + 1½ ounces vodka

BUBBLY SCREWDRIVER

½ ounce Prosecco Syrup (page 164) + 2 ounces vodka + 4 ounces orange juice

Drink Your Seasons

SPRING
Free Spirit Spritz (page 144)
Lillet Highball (page 51)
Rhubarb & Cognac Fizz (page 40)
Rosé All Day Spritz Punch (page 73)

SUMMER
Breakfast of Champions (page 36)
Fro-secco Spritz (page 62)
Frozen Peach Palmer (page 48)
Lemon Prosecco Pops (page 43)

FALL
The Apple-rol Spritz (page 65)
Persimmon Mezcal Sour (page 115)
Pumpkin-Spiced Irish Coffee (page 126)

WINTER
Kumquat Kick (page 52)
Nonna's Tom & Jerry (page 137)
Smoked Rosemary Negroni Sour (page 108)
Winter Sbagliato (page 66)
Winter Spice Sangria (page 120)

Drinks by Specialty Spirit

LICOR 43
La Dolce Vita (page 125)
Tiramisu Espresso-tini (page 133)

ELDERFLOWER LIQUEUR
Lychee Martini (page 111)

PASSION FRUIT LIQUEUR
Kentucky Jungle Bird (page 107)
Passion Fruit Martini (page 104)

CHILE LIQUEUR
Blood Orange Thyme Margarita (page 93)
Kumquat Kick (page 52)
Spicy Watermelon Punch (page 55)

AMARETTO
Apricot French 75 (page 103)
Lemon Meringue Martini (page 134)

LILLET
Lillet Highball (page 51)
Rosé All Day Spritz Punch (page 73)

CAMPARI
Kentucky Jungle Bird (page 107)
Smoked Rosemary Negroni Sour (page 108)
Sunset Spritz (page 70)
Winter Sbagliato (page 66)

APEROL
Citrus Party Punch Spritz (page 74)
Coconut Aperol Margarita (page 81)
Fro-secco Spritz (page 62)
Jules's Aperol Spritz (page 58)
The Apple-rol Spritz (page 65)

GREEN CHARTREUSE
Après Ski Hot Chocolate (page 130)
The Vacationer's Last Word (page 116)

Acknowledgments

To the widely talented (and patient) photographer and supportive sister, Lucianna McIntosh. I wouldn't be here if you hadn't pushed me to start Join Jules, let alone write a whole cocktail recipe book. For everything since the beginning, I am eternally grateful. I owe this book to you.

To my editor Raquel Pelzel and the Clarkson Potter team; thank you for being there every step of the way and bringing this beautiful book to life from start to finish.

To my agent, Andrianna deLone. I mean this, I wouldn't be here without you. Thank you for believing in me as a first time writer, for always calming my nerves and for being such a supportive force to help bring this dream to life.

To Anna Hezel, thank you for your invaluable involvement in this book. You have helped transform the pages of this book, making the art of home cocktailing not just accessible, but truly enjoyable.

To the creative team at Proplink studios, Nidia Cueva, David Peng, Caroline Hwang, and my illustrator Karl-Joel Larsson. Thank you for working with me and keeping me sane during the creative process, I wouldn't have captured the essence of this book without you all. A heartfelt thank you to each and every one of you for lending your artistic flair to this project.

To family: Mom, Dad, Uncle Brad, and Sina Reynosa-Poole. Thank you for your constant support and patience; it has been the bedrock of both this cocktail career and now cocktail book.

To my followers, I owe this to you. Thank you for following along in this journey, for every recipe made, and for helping build this community. Each one of you has played an indispensable role in building my career and making this book a reality, and for that I will forever be grateful.

Last, and most important, to my life partner and my biggest supporter, Eric Webber. Thank you will never be enough. Your constant support and belief in me have helped keep all this together. Thank you for always bearing with me and for always being my favorite drinking partner.

Here's to raising a glass to each and every one of you.

Xoxo, cheers!

Remember to always make it how you like, if it's not fresh we don't want it, and always garnish your cocktails because you deserve it!

Index

Page references in *italics* indicate photographs.

A

Amaretto
  Apricot French 75, *102*, 103
  Lemon Meringue Martini, 134, *135*
Amaro
  La Dolce Vita, *124*, 125
Aperol
  The Apple-rol Spritz, *64*, 65
  Citrus Party Punch Spritz, 74, *75*
  Coconut Margarita, *80*, 81
  Fro-secco Spritz, 62, *63*
  Spritz, Jules's, 58, *59*
Apple cider
  The Apple-rol Spritz, *64*, 65
  Winter Spice Sangria, 120, *121*
Apricot French 75, *102*, 103
Avocado Margarita, *84*, 85

B

Barspoon, 19
Basil
  & Bourbon Smash, *38*, 39
  Herbaceous Syrups, 162
  Stone Fruit Whiskey Sour, 112, *113*
Bitter liqueurs, 16
Bitters, 31
Blender, 19
Booze-free drinks, list of, 5
Bourbon, 15
  The Apple-rol Spritz, *64*, 65
  & Basil Smash, *38*, 39
  Freezer Door Manhattan, *128*, 129
  Frozen Peach Palmer, 48, *49*
  Kentucky Jungle Bird, *106*, 107
  Stone Fruit Whiskey Sour, 112, *113*
  Weekenders' Party Punch, *118*, 119
Brandy, 16
Brûléed garnish, 29

C

Campari
  Kentucky Jungle Bird, *106*, 107
  Smoked Rosemary Negroni Sour, 108, *109*
  Sunset Spritz, 70, *71*
  Winter Sbagliato, 66, *67*

Carajillo, Nonalcoholic, 152, *153*
Carrot Margarita, 86, *87*
Cherry Syrup, 161
Chile liqueur
  Blood Orange Thyme Margarita, *92*, 93
  Chile Liqueur, 167
  Kumquat Kick, 52, *53*
  Spicy Watermelon Punch, *54*, 55
Chocolate
  Hot, Après Ski, 130, *131*
  Tiramisu Espresso-tini, *132*, 133
Cinnamon Syrup, 163
Citrus juicer, 18
Club soda, 17
Cocktails
  bar tools, 18–19
  common categories, 12–13
  conversion sheet, 20
  elements of, 12
  glassware, 22–25
  scaling up, 20
  seasonal, list of, 169
  seasonal flavors, 10
  by specialty spirits, 169
  spirits for, 14–17
  three-ingredient, 168
Cocktail shaker, 18
Coconut
  Aperol Margarita, *80*, 81
  Jules's Piña Colada, *44*, 45
  Orange Dreamsicle, *142*, 143
  The Pink Daiquiri, *46*, 47
  Tiki Tiki Tiki Room, *154*, 155
Coffee
  Nonalcoholic Carajillo, 152, *153*
  Pumpkin-Spiced Irish, 126, *127*
  Tiramisu Espresso-tini, *132*, 133
Cognac, 16
Cognac & Rhubarb Fizz, 40, *41*
Cranberry
  Free Spirit Spritz, 144, *145*
  Syrup, 166
  Winter Sbagliato, 66, *67*
Cucumber
  Garden Refresher Punch, 156, *157*
  Syrup, 165
  The Verde Maria, *34*, 35

D

Daiquiri, The Pink, *46*, 47

E

Edible flowers, 31
Eggs
    Nonna's Tom & Jerry, *136*, 137
Elderflower liqueur
    Lychee Martini, *110*, 111
Everclear
    Homemade Citrus-cello, 138, *139*

F

Flaming garnish, 29–31
Flowers, edible, 31
French 75, Apricot, *102*, 103
Frosted glass, 28
Fruit. *See also specific fruits*
    Stone, Whiskey Sour, 112, *113*
    Winter Spice Sangria, 120, *121*

G

Garnishes, 28–31
Gin, 15
    Apricot French 75, *102*, 103
    Breakfast of Champions, 36, *37*
    Citrus Party Punch Spritz, 74, *75*
    Minus the, & Tonic, 148, *149*
    Olive Oil Martini, 100, *101*
    Smoked Rosemary Negroni Sour, 108, *109*
Glassware, 22–25
Grapefruit
    The Paloma-rita Sour, 90, *91*
    Sunset Spritz, 70, *71*
    Tiki Tiki Tiki Room, *154*, 155
    Weekenders' Party Punch, *118*, 119
Green chartreuse
    Après Ski Hot Chocolate, 130, *131*
    The Vacationer's Last Word, 116, *117*

H

Hand frother, 19
Herbs. *See also specific herbs*
    Herbaceous Syrups, 162
Highball, Lillet, *50*, 51
Honey Syrup, 160

I

Ice, 26
Irish whiskey, 15
    Pumpkin-Spiced Irish Coffee, 126, *127*

J

Jigger, 18
Jungle Bird, Kentucky, *106*, 107

K

Kitchen torch, 19
Kumquat Kick, 52, *53*

L

La Dolce Vita, *124*, 125
Lavender
    Garden Refresher Punch, 156, *157*
    Herbaceous Syrups, 162
Lemon
    Homemade Citrus-cello, 138, *139*
    Meringue Martini, 134, *135*
    Prosecco Pops, *42*, 43
Licor 43
    La Dolce Vita, *124*, 125
    Tiramisu Espresso-tini, *132*, 133
Lillet
    Highball, *50*, 51
    Rosé All Day Spritz Punch, *72*, 73
Lime
    Classic Margarita, 78, *79*
    Garden Refresher Punch, 156, *157*
    Melon No-jito, *150*, 151
    Pantry Margarita, 94, *95*
Limoncello
    Homemade Citrus-cello, 138, *139*
    Lemon Meringue Martini, 134, *135*
    Spritz, *60*, 61
Liqueurs, flavored, 17
Lychee Martini, *110*, 111

M

Mango
  Blended Tropical Margarita, *88*, 89
  Fro-secco Spritz, 62, *63*
Manhattan, Freezer Door, *128*, 129
Margarita, Booze-Free, *146*, 147
Margaritas, list of, 4
Martinis
  Lemon Meringue, 134, *135*
  Lychee, *110*, 111
  Olive Oil, 100, *101*
  Passion Fruit, 104, *105*
Melon No-jito, *150*, 151
Mezcal, 14
  Après Ski Hot Chocolate, 130, *131*
  Blood Orange Thyme Margarita, *92*, 93
  The Paloma-rita Sour, 90, *91*
  Persimmon Sour, *114*, 115
  Pineapple Margarita, 82, *83*
Mint
  Melon No-jito, *150*, 151
Mixing glass, 18
Muddler, 19

O

Olives
  Bianco Spritz, *68*, 69
  Olive Oil Martini, 100, *101*
Orange
  Blood, Thyme Margarita, *92*, 93
  Booze-Free Margarita, *146*, 147
  Citrus Party Punch Spritz, 74, *75*
  Dreamsicle, *142*, 143
  Free Spirit Spritz, 144, *145*
  Fro-secco Spritz, 62, *63*
  Homemade Citrus-cello, 138, *139*
  Kumquat Kick, 52, *53*
  Nonalcoholic Carajillo, 152, *153*
  Weekenders' Party Punch, *118*, 119
  Zest Syrup, 164
Orange liqueur
  Avocado Margarita, *84*, 85
  Blended Tropical Margarita, *88*, 89
  Carrot Margarita, 86, *87*
  Classic Margarita, 78, *79*
  Coconut Aperol Margarita, *80*, 81
  The Paloma-rita Sour, 90, *91*
  Pantry Margarita, 94, *95*
  Pineapple Mezcal Margarita, 82, *83*

  Tangy Tamarind Punch, *96*, 97
  Winter Spice Sangria, 120, *121*

P

The Paloma-rita Sour, 90, *91*
Passion fruit liqueur
  Kentucky Jungle Bird, *106*, 107
  Passion Fruit Martini, 104, *105*
Passion Fruit Martini, 104, *105*
Peach Palmer, Frozen, 48, *49*
Peelers, 19
Pepper(s)
  Spicy, Syrup, 166
  The Verde Maria, *34*, 35
Persimmon
  Mezcal Sour, *114*, 115
  Syrup, 165
Piña Colada, Jules's, 44, *45*
Pineapple
  Blended Tropical Margarita, *88*, 89
  Jules's Piña Colada, 44, *45*
  Kentucky Jungle Bird, *106*, 107
  Mezcal Margarita, 82, *83*
  Passion Fruit Martini, 104, *105*
  Tiki Tiki Tiki Room, *154*, 155
Pops, Lemon Prosecco, *42*, 43
Prosecco
  Bianco Spritz, *68*, 69
  Citrus Party Punch Spritz, 74, *75*
  Fro-secco Spritz, 62, *63*
  Jules's Aperol Spritz, 58, *59*
  Lemon Pops, *42*, 43
  Limoncello Spritz, 60, *61*
  Syrup, 164
  Winter Sbagliato, 66, *67*
Pumpkin
  -Spiced Irish Coffee, 126, *127*
  Spice Syrup, 162

R

Rhubarb
  & Cognac Fizz, 40, *41*
  Free Spirit Spritz, 144, *145*
  Shrub, 167
Rimmed glass, 28
Rosé All Day Spritz Punch, *72*, 73
Rosemary
  Herbaceous Syrups, 162
  Smoked, Negroni Sour, 108, *109*

Rum, 16
    Jules's Piña Colada, 44, 45
    La Dolce Vita, 124, 125
    Nonna's Tom & Jerry, 136, 137
    The Pink Daiquiri, 46, 47
    The Vacationer's Last Word, 116, 117
Rye whiskey, 15

S

Sangria, Winter Spice, 120, 121
Scotch, 15
Shrub, Rhubarb, 167
Simple Syrup, Plain, 160
Sparkling water, 17
Sparkling wine, 17. See also Prosecco
    The Apple-rol Spritz, 64, 65
    Apricot French 75, 102, 103
    Rosé All Day Spritz Punch, 72, 73
    The Vacationer's Last Word, 116, 117
    Weekenders' Party Punch, 118, 119
Spritz, Free Spirit, 144, 145
Spritzes, list of, 4
Strainer, 18
Strawberry
    Breakfast of Champions, 36, 37
    Coconut Aperol Margarita, 80, 81
    The Pink Daiquiri, 46, 47
    Rosé All Day Spritz Punch, 72, 73
    Syrup, 161
Swath, 28
Syrups, list of, 5

T

Tamarind Punch, Tangy, 96, 97
Tea
    Frozen Peach Palmer, 48, 49
Tequila, 14
    Avocado Margarita, 84, 85
    Blended Tropical Margarita, 88, 89
    Carrot Margarita, 86, 87
    Classic Margarita, 78, 79
    Coconut Aperol Margarita, 80, 81
    The Paloma-rita Sour, 90, 91
    Pantry Margarita, 94, 95
    Tangy Tamarind Punch, 96, 97
    The Verde Maria, 34, 35
Tequila alternative
    Booze-Free Margarita, 146, 147

Thyme
    Blood Orange Margarita, 92, 93
    Herbaceous Syrups, 162
Tomatillos
    The Verde Maria, 34, 35
Tom & Jerry, Nonna's, 136, 137
Tonic water, 17
Twist, 28

V

Vanilla-Cinnamon Syrup, 163
Vanilla Syrup, 163
The Verde Maria, 34, 35
Vermouth, 16–17
    Bianco Spritz, 68, 69
    Freezer Door Manhattan, 128, 129
    Olive Oil Martini, 100, 101
    Smoked Rosemary Negroni Sour, 108, 109
    Winter Sbagliato, 66, 67
Vodka, 14
    Chile Liqueur, 167
    Homemade Citrus-cello, 138, 139
    Lemon Meringue Martini, 134, 135
    Lychee Martini, 110, 111
    Olive Oil Martini, 100, 101
    Passion Fruit Martini, 104, 105
    Spicy Watermelon Punch, 54, 55
    Tiramisu Espresso-tini, 132, 133

W

Watermelon Punch, Spicy, 54, 55
Wheels and wedges, 28–29
Whiskey, 15
Whiskey Sour, Stone Fruit, 112, 113
Wine. See also Sparkling wine
    Sunset Spritz, 70, 71
    Winter Spice Sangria, 120, 121

Y

Yogurt
    Breakfast of Champions, 36, 37

Z

Zesters, 19

Library of Congress Cataloging-in-Publication Data
Names: McIntosh, Julianna, author. | McIntosh,
Lucianna, photographer.
Title: Pretty simple cocktails / Julianna McIntosh;
photographs by Lucianna McIntosh.
Identifiers: LCCN 2024002872 (print) | LCCN
2024002873 (ebook) | ISBN 9780593582022 (hard-
cover) | ISBN 9780593582039 (ebook) Subjects:
LCSH: Cocktails. | LCGFT: Cookbooks.
Classification: LCC TX951 .M3475 2024 (print) | LCC
TX951 (ebook) | DDC 641.87/4—dc23/eng/20240212
LC record available at
https://lccn.loc.gov/2024002872
LC ebook record available at
https://lccn.loc.gov/2024002873

ISBN 978-0-593-58202-2
Ebook ISBN 978-0-593-58203-9

Printed in China

Editor: Raquel Pelzel
Editorial assistant: Elaine Hennig
Designer: Robert Diaz
Production editor: Natalie Blachere
Production manager: Jessica Heim
Compositors: Merri Ann Morrell,
Hannah Hunt, and Zoe Tokushige
Copyeditor: Kate Slate
Proofreader: Jacob Sammon
Indexer: Elizabeth Parson
Marketer: Joey Lozada
Publicist: Jina Stanfill

Illustrations by Karl-Joel Larsson

10 9 8 7 6 5 4 3 2 1

First Edition

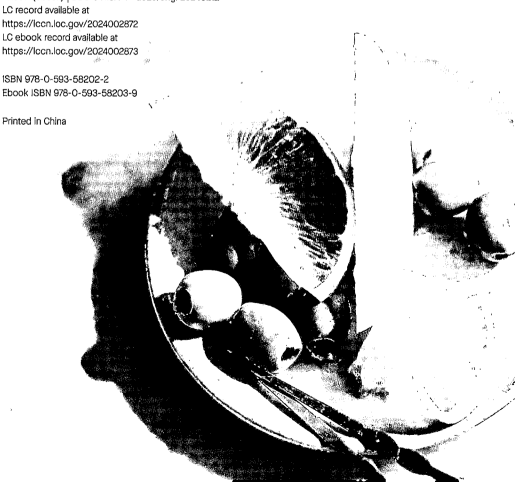

Clarkson Potter/Publishers
New York
clarksonpotter.com

Cover design: **ROBERT DIAZ**
Cover photographs: **LUCIANNA MCINTOSH**